Understanding the Cultures
of the Middle East

Economy, Trade, and Resources across the Middle East

Tatiana Ryckman

Cavendish
Square

New York

Published in 2017 by Cavendish Square Publishing, LLC
243 5th Avenue, Suite 136, New York, NY 10016

Copyright © 2017 by Cavendish Square Publishing, LLC

First Edition

CPSIA Compliance Information: Batch #CW17CSQ

All websites were available and accurate when this book was sent to press.

Library of Congress Cataloging-in-Publication Data

Names: Ryckman, Tatiana.
Title: Economy, trade, and resources across the Middle East / Tatiana Ryckman.
Description: New York : Cavendish Square Publishing, 2017. | Series: Understanding the cultures of the Middle East | Includes index.
Identifiers: ISBN 9781502623706 (library bound) | ISBN 9781502623713 (ebook)
Subjects: LCSH: Middle East--Economic conditions--Juvenile literature. | Middle East--Juvenile literature.
Classification: LCC DS44.R93 2017 | DDC 956--dc23

Editorial Director: David McNamara
Editor: Elizabeth Schmermund
Copy Editor: Rebecca Rohan
Associate Art Director: Amy Greenan
Designer: Alan Sliwinski
Production Coordinator: Karol Szymczuk
Photo Research: J8 Media

Contents

Introduction 5

1 The History of the Economy
   across the Middle East 11

2 The Modern-Day Economy in the Gulf 27

3 The Modern-Day Economy
   in the Levant Region 53

4 The Modern-Day Economy
   in North Africa 71

5 Important Figures in the Economy
   across the Middle East 83

Chronology 98

Map of the Region 100

Glossary 102

Further Information 104

Bibliography 106

Index 110

About the Author 112

The economy of the Middle East is dependent on many resources and the political climate of each individual country.

Introduction

The term Middle East was first used by early colonialists, or people who sought territory in a nation other than their own, seeking to differentiate between the *near* East (including Turkey and Cyprus), the *middle* East, and the *far* East (China). Far from a perfect moniker, this shorthand lumped together countless cultures, ethnicities, and languages. Our modern definition of the Middle East refers to a vast expanse of 3,500,000 square miles (9,064,958 square kilometers), 19 countries, and over 350 million people. Because the region encompasses so much diversity, it's impossible to talk about the

Middle East as having a single history, religion, political system, or economy.

Economic prosperity is measured with a number of factors, such as natural resources, industry, imports, and exports. But even these factors play into a larger set of interdependent factors that affect a nation's economy. Other contributing factors to take into account when studying a nation's prosperity include its gross national income (GNI), which indicates how much money a country makes; the democracy index, which ranks a nation's political system according to its degree of democracy and is often tied to its level of political and economic stability; foreign relations, which influence a nation's ability to trade and therefore also affects its national income; and **modernization**, which includes everything from an educated workforce to maintaining relevant industries that can compete in a world market.

There are still more peripheral elements that may influence a nation's economic well-being. Political unrest and disputes based on religion or ethnicity can all disrupt a country's internal productivity as well as its relationships with other countries. To further complicate matters, religious ties in the Middle East are enmeshed with ancient tribal identities and royal family histories, making it difficult to separate political, religious, familial, and cultural disputes.

The Middle East is a region of enormous wealth alongside striking poverty. Massive wealth from oil and natural gas resources has meant that wealth is distributed unevenly throughout the Middle East. The uneven distribution of resources has provoked distrust between nations and created enormous economic disparity between the wealthy families who own the oil and the workers, often poor migrants seeking jobs, who serve them.

But oil has had positive effects as well. When global oil prices are high, so are incomes in those countries—even for the large populations of **expatriate**, or foreign, professionals who move there for work. The most oil-rich countries also enjoy ultra-modern infrastructure and urban development, which not only promote tourism, foreign investment, and multicultural exchange, but help residents of those countries gain access to education and higher quality of life. It's hard to think of a place that so clearly exemplifies the old adage, "It takes money to make money."

However, it's impossible to say all nations of the Middle East enjoy the same abundance of natural resources, and even the most oil-rich countries understand that they are enjoying a limited commodity. Across the Middle East, there have been major initiatives to diversify economies. While Saudi Arabia, Iran, and Iraq are all still incredibly oil-dependent, they are also looking into more sustainable ways to increase their wealth and distribute it more evenly across their populations. Iran, for instance, has had one of the highest rates of growth in the sciences of any country in the world. Much of that research is in **hydrocarbons**—the chemical makeup of oil that makes it useful for producing energy— and it is making Iran a leader in a field the entire world depends on.

While the world's leading oil suppliers are preparing for the inevitable end of fossil fuels, other countries across the Middle East have had to find ways to facilitate their economies without large oil and natural gas deposits. Tunisia, for instance, has been building their manufacturing and banking sectors for decades,

Safety is a top concern for many countries in the Middle East that rely on tourism to increase their national income.

and both industries provide many jobs for citizens with a wide range of education levels and economic backgrounds. Other oil-poor countries in the Middle East have worked tirelessly to build their tourism industries. Many of the countries in the region have long coastlines perfect for beach resorts and ports that make the countries accessible for trade.

If it's hard for you to imagine vacationing in the Middle East, that's not surprising, given that the region is usually featured in Western media for its political conflicts. This international image is not lost on the people of the Middle East, and many nations have made great efforts to improve international relations. Morocco, for instance, has long acted as an ally to Western nations, aiding in the fight against terrorism. They have also started an initiative to double the tourism industry in their country by 2020, making stability and safety an invaluable asset to strive for. Conversely, Lebanon has also worked tirelessly to build its tourism industry in the wake of conflicts that demolished much of its infrastructure, but the Lebanese have struggled to recover as violence in neighboring Syria floods their country with refugees and wards off tourists afraid of possible danger.

As you can see, each nation in the Middle East has its own resources and challenges. Centuries of foreign rule, internal conflicts, and sudden wealth have made the region both rich and volatile. To understand the region's economy, one must understand the long history that led to its cultural identity both within its own borders and in relation to the world beyond.

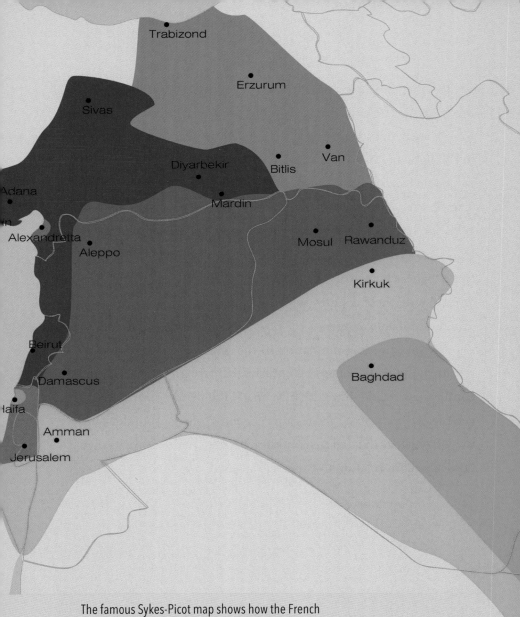

The famous Sykes-Picot map shows how the French
and English redrew the lines of the Middle East
without regard to the cultures or natural geographical
boundaries that make up the region. Here, dark blue
denotes French occupation, dark pink denotes British
occupation, and green denotes Russian occupation.
Light blue and light pink regions indicate French
and British protectorates, respectively, while purple
denotes international zones.

1

The History of the Economy across the Middle East

Indeed, while observers from other nations might see political corruption and religious fanaticism as the leading challenges in the region, the people who live there are concerned about the same issue that has caused revolutions throughout history: money.

But it is difficult to talk about the economic history of the Middle East without recognizing that the countries that make up this region have experienced many shifts in borders, leaders, and dominant religions over the last one hundred years. Additionally, this region's wealth of resources—first agriculture and later oil—has made it attractive to international investors and politicians. And this outside interest has been the source of centuries of conflict.

Where in the World

For the purposes of this book, the term "Middle East" covers a wide swath of land, reaching west to Morocco just south of Spain in the northwestern corner of Africa, and as far east as Iran on the eastern shore of the Persian Gulf.

Gulf Region

The Gulf region is made up of the countries surrounding the Persian Gulf and includes Oman, United Arab Emirates, Saudi Arabia, Yemen, Qatar, Bahrain, Kuwait, Iraq, and Iran. This region is known for its wealth of oil deposits, upon which many of these countries depend for their economic well-being. Because of the arid landscape it can be difficult to grow crops, making these countries incredibly expensive to live in. In countries such as Qatar and the United Arab Emirates, this is rarely a problem for nationals who live there because of their ancestral ties to the land and ruling families, but for the millions of expatriate workers, fresh produce can be prohibitively expensive. This dichotomy results in a stark contrast between the extreme wealth between those who enjoy the unimaginable luxury of cities like Dubai and the poverty of the migrant workers who built the city.

Thanks to natural beaches along the Persian Gulf and enormous oil wealth, the United Arab Emirates has been able to build lucrative tourist destinations.

For countries like Bahrain who have seen their hydrocarbon, or fossil fuel, resources become increasingly scarce, a big push has been made toward diversifying industry. For Iran, this has meant a focus on education and technological developments. As a result, Iran has educated some of the greatest concentrations of scientists in the region but also struggles with a phenomenon known as **brain drain**, which is when the highest-educated members of a population leave for opportunities elsewhere. This isn't just a problem because of fewer educated citizens, but because it can stunt innovation and economic growth.

A major resource in this region is the gulf itself, which provides ports so the oil-rich nations can export hydrocarbons to buyers all over the world. And for countries seeking new revenue streams, the gulf beaches provide valuable income as tourist attractions.

Levant Region

The countries of the Levant region include Egypt, Jordan, Lebanon, Israel, Palestine, and Syria. You may recognize many of these countries from the news as Syria struggles through a civil war and the Palestinian/Israeli conflict continues. Lebanon has also been adversely affected by the Syrian war, but its unique history as a former French territory has made Lebanese nationals valuable abroad because they often speak many languages.

Jordan has used its geographical significance as the land at the heart of these two conflicts as a means to broker peace among these populations as well as abroad. This important role has encouraged countries all over the world to trust Jordan and invest in their economy, making them one of the most stable countries in the area. Egypt has also seen economic growth as they diversify their resources away from oil and into other sectors.

North Africa

Morocco, Algeria, Libya, and Tunisia comprise the North African region of the Middle East. Though they each have their own tumultuous history, these countries have been relatively prosperous. Just across the Strait of Gibraltar from Spain, Morocco has been influenced by Europe for centuries. But, just as importantly, they have insisted on independence and developed their own culture and system of government. Neighboring Algeria was also ruled by the French in the wake of the World Wars. Indeed, Algeria has a long history of occupation, dating back to the Romans. Today, however, the nation enjoys its independence and is the biggest country on the continent.

Tunisia lies to the northeast of Algeria, and though it is relatively small, boasts an impressive culture and economy. This is thanks, in part, to the leadership of the country's first president, Habib Bourguiba, who led the Tunisian rebellion against the French occupation of their country in the 1950s and worked explicitly to improve women's rights and education. Libya is nearly 680,000 square miles (1,761,192 sq. km)—roughly the size of Illinois, Missouri, Arkansas, Oklahoma, Kansas, and Nebraska all together—and shares its western border with Algeria and Tunisia, and its eastern border with Egypt.

The First and Second World Wars

The first and second World Wars played an important role in the development of Middle Eastern nations. As the European powers redrew the boundaries of the Middle East, disassembling the Ottoman Empire, many nations were mapped without regard to geographic landmarks or the ethnicities, beliefs, and cultures each new country contained. In fact, many of the region's conflicts today are still blamed on this map drawn by European powers.

Life Before the World War(s)

Each of the countries outlined in this book has its own individual history and background. Many of them flourished in ancient times as part of the Roman or Persian empires on various trade routes.

This region also benefitted from the **Golden Age of Islam**. During this period, from the eighth to thirteenth centuries, Islamic nations celebrated the shared knowledge made possible by their practice of the **hajj**, or the pilgrimage to Mecca, which is a fundamental pillar of Islam. This included enormous leaps in medical and scientific knowledge and architectural innovation, as well as the dissemination of literature and art. Because so many nationalities came together at Mecca, Muslims would exchange ideas and even texts, which allowed for works to be translated and shared across cultures. Our modern banking system is even based on innovations in moneylending that developed in the region during this time.

The **Ottoman Empire**, also called the Turkish Empire, began in 1299 and spread first under the rule of Osman I, and later under Murad I in the 1300s. In the sixteenth and seventeenth centuries, the Ottoman Empire reached the peak of its power, spreading from southeastern Europe, south to North Africa, and east to western Asia. But as Europe gained power in the nineteenth century, the Ottoman Empire began to decline.

Though the exact cause of World War I is disputed, it is widely agreed that it was initiated by the assassination of Archduke Franz Ferdinand of Austria and his wife, Sophie, Duchess of Hohenburg. Continued economic, territorial, and nationalist disputes between two powerful groups of allies (Germany and Austria-Hungary, with whom the Ottoman Empire allied, on one side and Russia, France, Serbia, and Great Britain on the other) became entangled with the **power vacuum** created by the Ottoman Empire's decline.

The Sykes-Picot Agreement

As European powers carved up the failing Ottoman Empire, they also redrew the boundaries of their new territories. In May 1916, Britain and France secretly agreed to divvy up the territories of the Middle East between themselves at the end of the First World War, although they had previously agreed to grant these territories independence. This became known as the **Sykes-Picot Agreement**.

This agreement had many effects, including European powers deliberately blocking the development of infrastructure that would connect the territories of the Middle East. This choice was made to deliberately stop the Ottoman Empire from efficiently mobilizing troops, but stunting the growth of these states has had lasting effects. Furthermore, the British planned to attack the weakened Ottomans in order to get them out of the war altogether, and improve their own chance of winning and taking over the Middle Eastern region.

But simply "undoing" the damage wrought by the Sykes-Picot borders by redrawing them poses new problems, chief among them the fact that Arabs suspect international interest in new borders as being foreign plots to divide and weaken them all over again.

Though it would seem that the French and British simply claimed the Middle East as their own without a fight from the people who lived in that region, that's not exactly the case. The British had begun negotiations with Arab leaders, promising them expansive empires if they would help overthrow the Turks. This was proposed as an opportunity for long-awaited independence for the Arab world, with the exception of a few territories that would be offered as spoils, or rewards, for France and Britain's assistance in liberating them. As you'll read in the following chapters, that's not exactly what happened.

Life after World War II

After nearly three decades of European influence, the majority of people in the Middle East grew frustrated with European governance. As Tarek Osman reported for the BBC:

> When ... independence did not materialize after World War One, and as these colonial powers ... continued to exert immense influence over the Arab world, the thrust of Arab politics ... gradually but decisively shifted from building liberal constitutional governance systems (as Egypt, Syria, and Iraq had witnessed in the early decades of the twentieth century) to assertive **nationalism** whose main objective was getting rid of the colonialists and the ruling systems that worked with them.

President Gamal Abdel Nasser of Egypt was a key figure in uniting the Arab people in their fight for independence against colonialist influence in the wake of World War II. Many leaders across the Middle East were inspired by Nasser's unlikely rise to power and dogged loyalty to the pursuit of independence. In fact, all across the region new leaders stood up to unify their countries in search of independence and a national identity.

During World War II, the Camel Corps of the Arab Legion unified to stave off Europeans seeking to claim the Middle East.

As the European powers reluctantly withdrew, the newly independent nations in the Middle East were faced with a new quandary: How would their newly sovereign nations fit into the rest of the world?

New national economies struggled through the nineteenth and twentieth centuries to effectively build their infrastructure and economy, and to modernize so they could join an international market and improve their standard of living. Great strides are still being made in public education and diversification of industry, and many countries in the Middle East enjoy the riches associated with vast natural resources, such as oil, natural gas, and minerals.

Even with these steps toward progress, continued Western presence and control over resources have made Middle Eastern populations wary of foreign investment and even aid. As these populations experience rapid growth, the uneven distribution of wealth and vital resources (like water) create conflicts. The repeated clash of objectives and ideology has led to high military spending and economic instability.

Modernization Versus Westernization

Until borders were redrawn by colonialists in the wake of the World Wars, many of the countries in the Middle East were resistant to change, including both **westernization** and modernization. Though these terms are often used interchangeably, this inaccurately implies that the West is uniformly modern and better off than nations of the East, ignoring the many technological, scientific, and medical advancements that are the gifts of the East. Rather, westernization refers to the ways in which other nations emulate Western culture and beliefs, while modernization refers to a nation's ability to join the world market and adapt to new technologies.

Indeed, many Middle Eastern countries were slow to modernize. Leading up to World War I, private businesses in the region were small and seldom outlived their founders. Today, businesses boast how long they've been in operation to communicate to their customers that their company is trustworthy. But for a long time this was not a concern for businessmen throughout the Middle East. Partnerships and alliances were formed only to accomplish a specific task, such as pooling resources to purchase a large shipment of cargo at a lower bulk price, or in order to split the shipping cost of many items, and then their alliance would end.

This is where the line between westernization and modernization blur, because while communities in the Middle East were still operating on a local level with little longevity, the countries of the West were establishing modern banking institutions and professional practices intended to grow and last for generations. These large companies made it easier to mobilize funds and improve efficiency by delegating specific tasks to different specialized workers. The most famous example of this form of modern industrialization is Henry Ford's assembly line, which cut the time it took to build a car down from twelve hours to two. This not only allowed Ford cars to dominate the automotive industry of their time but has helped them stay in business ever since.

But for the Middle East to join the world in economic modernity did not necessitate an unchecked acceptance of all aspects of Western culture. Timur Kuran, professor of economics and political studies at Duke University, wrote in 2004:

> *The modernization theorists of the mid-twentieth century ... erred also in equating these two concepts. To them, economic modernization entailed the wholesale adoption of western institutions and beliefs. Here the concept has a narrower meaning. Consisting of institutional changes to support economic transactions of rising scale, duration, and complexity, and to provide economic actors greater flexibility, modernizing economic reforms are vehicles for catching up with the wealthiest countries in productivity and consumption. They need not amount to blind imitation or eradication of differences.*

The US–Middle East Partnership Initiative (MEPI)

The United States State Department encourages citizens of various Middle Eastern and North African countries to build stronger communities both today and in the future.

The program boasts: "MEPI exchange programs enhance cultural understanding, international collaboration, democratic institution building, knowledge sharing, and economic development between US- and Middle East/North Africa-based students, entrepreneurs, lawmakers, and civil society leaders."

Though the program benefits from federal aid, the projects MEPI participates in are largely in the civil sector, and the program prides itself on its mission of civilian empowerment. This is possibly the most important aspect of the exchange, because it provides local civilians with the resources to solve the issues most important to them. Like the old adage, "Give a man a fish, feed him for a day, teach a man to fish, feed him for a lifetime," this model gives individual members of a community the agency and ability to learn new skills and meet their goals. The issues that this program supports are usually to safeguard and progress civil liberties and human rights.

MEPI also provides a path for students to experience crosscultural exchange between the United States and the Middle East. This promotes understanding between these different cultures and lays the foundation for future stability.

Making a Nation

Nationalism, the patriotic feelings of loyalty to one nation over others, is a relatively recent phenomenon. The French Revolution in the late 1700s was one of the first instances of nationalism and gave rise to feelings of national pride across Europe. This helped define the identities of those nations as they sought independence and began interacting with other countries in political and economic spheres.

Late in the nineteenth century, as Middle Eastern states fought against the expanding Ottoman Empire, Middle Eastern Christians—who sometimes had greater exposure to European influence—began to form nationalist groups. Iran and Egypt were at the forefront of nationalist movements in the region. In northern Africa wealthy Egyptians sought to rule their own country—long ruled by an Ottoman family—and promoted their ideals under the slogan "Egypt for the Egyptians." Further East, in the Gulf region, Iranians also advocated for independence, a movement which led to a new constitutional government in the early 1900s. As European nations began infiltrating Middle Eastern politics, the cultures collided. Nationalism was a catalyst for independence from Europe, but European nationalist identities set a precedent in these new, developing countries. Patriotism was a new idea that slowly spread around the globe.

Catching Up to the Past

The long road from colonialism to independence left a bitter taste for these new independent nations, and the region's long history of occupation has had a lasting effect.

Many nations in the Middle East have flourished with their new wealth from fossil fuels but have been careful to maintain their rich history as they build new infrastructure. An example is the Burj Al Arab hotel off the coast of the United Arab Emirates—the tallest hotel in the world.

Trial and Error

To further wean themselves from foreign involvement and dependence on Western goods, many of the new governments implemented a strategy known as **import-substituting industrialization (ISI)**. By introducing trade barriers and **subsidizing** new industries in their own countries, the governments hoped to rapidly grow the local economy while reducing importation of foreign goods. Ultimately, ISI failed because the industry subsidies offered by the government gradually grew, until many businesses were state-owned and riddled with corruption and bureaucracy that rendered them ineffective to the populations they were meant to serve.

When ISI proved an insufficient way to grow new economic wealth, Egypt's president, Anwar Sadat, tried an **infitah** policy, which literally translates to "open door." In what seems like a total reversal of ideology, Middle Eastern countries began seeking foreign investment in the 1970s. Western nations quickly moved in to invest in oil and technology, bringing with them fast food chains and name brand clothing. Rather than bolster local economic development, this westernization has had the opposite effect by intensifying the economic gap between the wealthy who can afford Western luxuries and the poorer masses, and by replacing long-held traditions.

What Lay Ahead

The negative impact of Western influence on Middle Eastern cultures and economies has fed into the growing number of radical Islamic opposition groups. While these militant religious groups have taken center stage internationally, they also influence local politics, sometimes creating instability in their home or neighboring countries. Conflicting political, military, and religious entities have had a profound effect on the economy of each state as well as the whole region. This is exemplified in Palestine's struggle for land, jobs, and education as Israel increases its holdings in what was once a shared territory. Further east, in Syria, antigovernment protests have resulted in over four million deaths and millions more displaced citizens. Not surprisingly, these conflicts have discouraged businesses and tourists from coming to the country as well as neighboring countries, like Lebanon.

Even as conflicts persist, it is negligent to assume all of the countries of the Middle East are the same. While many of them face similar challenges, the resources, policies, and educational systems of each nation create a varied cultural and economic patchwork across the Middle East.

The countries of the Gulf Region make up half of the top ten oil producers in the world, making this region a hotbed of economic activity.

2

The Modern-Day Economy in the Gulf

When you read about the Middle East, the Gulf region is likely the territory that comes to mind. These territories include the ring of countries surrounding the Persian Gulf. Oman and the United Arab Emirates (UAE) are on the southwestern coast of the gulf, and to the south of Saudi Arabia. Further north on the western side of the gulf lie Qatar and Bahrain, with Kuwait, Iraq, and Iran cupping the northern tip of this invaluable waterway. This may have to do with the perpetual War on Terror, which has increased Western, and specifically American, awareness of this area and its complicated religious, political, and economic climate.

Some of these oil-rich countries have had turbulent relationships with each other as well as the wider international community. At the same time, they often depend on one another for basic resources such as food, even while their large deposits of fossil fuels compete on the world market.

Bahrain

Once a British protectorate (like many of the countries along the Gulf coast of the Arabian Peninsula), Bahrain gained independence when its treaty with Britain expired in 1971. At the same time, oil reserves were running low, forcing the new nation to diversify its economy quickly.

Bahrain, an archipelago off of the Arabian Peninsula with islands in the Persian Gulf, has been in a difficult geographic location since its foundation. Originally called a state, Bahrain became a kingdom in 2002. Surrounded by large, oil-rich countries, Bahrainis have had to work doubly hard to maintain peaceful relationships among neighbors while also trying to compete with them for international business.

Resources, Commerce, and Trade

In 2006, Bahrain was reported to have the fastest growing population in the world. This is surprising, given that Bahrain is an island state with minimal oil reserves and a defunct pearl trade. The population of roughly 1.3 million is nearly half expatriate workers, many of whom come for construction jobs and menial labor—which may explain the startling gender discrepancy between the number of adult males (568,000) and females (308,000) in Bahrain.

So where is this rapid growth coming from? While oil supplies have slowed, they still account for 60 percent of exports and 70 percent of government revenues. Second to fossil fuels are financial services, which London's Global Financial Centres Index named the fastest growing in the world. Another large export for Bahrain is construction materials, a valuable commodity as wealthy nearby countries like Qatar, Saudi Arabia, and the UAE build new, elaborate buildings and continue to develop infrastructure.

The nation has also capitalized on its most obvious feature: it is a series of islands, attractive to tourists. The islands boast exotic wild life and great biodiversity, with hundreds of species of migratory birds.

For the people who live in Bahrain, including the many expats who move there for work, the booming economy has improved quality of life. Great strides in human rights were made in 1999 as well, when the present king, Emir Hamad al-Khalifa, succeeded his father as ruler. Upon becoming king, Hamad al-Khalifa imposed new laws against torture and, by 2002, women had the right to vote. Unfortunately, in the wake of the political and religious protests throughout the Middle East since 2011, torture was reinstituted. Furthermore, female leaders, such as Haya Rashed al-Khalifa, Bahrain's first-ever female ambassador, have complained that the government's social reforms are artificial and not reaching the lives of women outside of the government.

The Gulf War

In 1990, Iraqi dictator Saddam Hussein ordered the invasion of Kuwait. Iraq was still struggling under crippling debt left over from the Iran-Iraq war and saw Saudi Arabia's and Kuwait's high oil production as a deliberate tactic to keep oil prices low, stunting Iraq's economic growth.

This political cartoon of Saddam Hussein sitting on a powder keg suggests the imminent threat that unrest in the Gulf Region posed to the rest of the world.

By 1991, the United States feared that Saudi Arabia would be Iraq's next target, disrupting the leading supply of oil to the entire world. This led to Operation Desert Storm, a one-hundred-hour, US-led attack on Iraq, resulting in Iraq's retreat. As Iraqis pulled out of Kuwait, they set fire to nearly six hundred oil wells across the country.

Though the conflict was relatively brief, it has had lasting implications for the economies of the involved nations. It is estimated that eleven million barrels of oil were released in the Persian Gulf during the conflict, which was an enormous economic loss, not just for the oil, but because it contaminated water and decimated agricultural land. The trade embargos instituted in Iraq as punishment for its part in the war decimated the country. Since then, Iraq has continued to suffer from debt and persistent conflict, as intellectuals and professionals seek stability and security in other countries. Similarly, Kuwait suffered substantial losses in oil and environmental damages, and gained debt and general instability.

Iran

Iran's vast expanse lies to the east of Iraq and encompasses the entire eastern coast of the Persian Gulf. Iran's western border is shared with Turkey and Iraq, while Turkmenistan, Afghanistan, and Pakistan lie to the east. The Caspian Sea creates a shore along the north of Iran, while the Persian Gulf makes up the southern coastline of the country.

Originally inhabited by the Proto-Elamite kingdom in 3200 BCE, this large country is home to one of the oldest existing cultures. Unlike its neighbors, Iran was never part of the Ottoman Empire, and though there have been waves of outside influence, Iran's strides toward independence look different from other countries in the region. Before the Ottoman Empire spread to the Middle East, the Persians ruled over much of the land. During the Achaemenid Empire in 550 BCE, Iran's power reached from Eastern Europe to China and encompassed many countries. It was the largest empire the world had ever known.

Islam came to Iran in 633 CE. Because Islam places such a high importance on the hajj, where people from all over the world meet and exchange ideas and cultures, Iran quickly joined other Islamic nations in innovation. During this **Islamic Golden Age**, the sciences and arts flourished.

In 1907, as the world industrialized and saw the development of the press and other means of modernization, the Iranian people sought governmental reforms via the Persian Constitutional Revolution, which resulted in a constitutional monarchy and a legislative body. In the 1950s, the United Kingdom and the

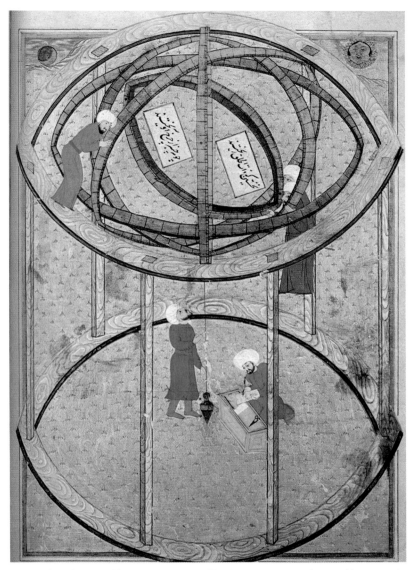

During the Islamic Golden Age, scientists, like the astronomers depicted here, made huge advances, including early medical textbooks and the development of math systems, like algebra.

United States orchestrated a coup d'état against a democratically elected Iranian leader, increasing Iranian distrust of foreign, and especially Western, influences.

By 1979, popular distrust for foreign influence spurred the Iranian Revolution and led to the formation of an Islamic Republic, a nation that blends Islamic beliefs with a modern government.

Resources, Commerce, and Trade

Because it supplies oil and gas to so many other countries, Iran is considered an energy superpower. Supplying fossil fuels to many other nations gives Iran control over the market—a benefit for them, and something to be wary of for those dependent on those resources.

The World Bank succinctly explains the state of Iran's economic affairs:

> Iran is the second largest economy in the Middle East … after Saudi Arabia, with an estimated **Gross Domestic Product (GDP)** in 2015 of US $393.7 billion … Iran's economy is characterized by a large hydrocarbon sector, small scale agriculture and services sectors, and a noticeable state presence in manufacturing and financial services. Iran ranks second in the world in natural gas reserves and fourth in proven crude oil reserves. Economic activity and government revenues still depend to a large extent on oil revenues and therefore remain volatile.

As we've seen in many other countries in the region, overreliance on a single resource—even one as valuable as oil—can lead to economic instability. The United States banned oil imports from Iran and put economic sanctions in place in 1979 after the Iranian Revolution. Since 2012, other countries, including the European Union, have also restricted trade and oil imports in response to Iran's nuclear programs, which they see as potentially dangerous. As a result, Iran has been surpassed in oil production by Iraq for the first time since the 1980s and it is estimated that Iran will lose $50 billion in oil revenue as a result.

But Iran is not dependent on hydrocarbons alone. In 2011, Iran had the highest rate of scientific growth in the world—this is especially impressive given the flight of educated elite who hope for a safer and more stable life elsewhere. Additionally, a deal was struck with the world powers regarding Iran's nuclear development in 2015 with plans for the removal of the main sanctions against Iran.

There are positive opportunities on the horizon for Iran. The World Bank reports:

> *Although growth is expected to be 1.7 percent this year, Iran's economy is expected to grow faster from 2016 onwards, following the agreement to limit nuclear development and allow more inspections of its nuclear sites. The lifting of sanctions—and Iran's return to the global economy—may bring an extra one million barrels of crude a day onto the international market, lowering global oil prices by about 13 percent. The lower prices are likely to hurt other oil exporters more than Iran, as the positive*

effect of higher oil production in Iran should outweigh the negative impact of falling global prices.

Iraq

After invading Afghanistan in 2001, the United States shifted its focus to Iraq in 2003. Rumors of weapons of mass destruction (WMDs) in Iraq led the United States to invade the country and overthrow the government led by Saddam Hussein. This led to great instability in Iraq and a rise of violence, and eventually a full-blown civil war, led by extremist groups.

Additionally, a mixed religious and ethnic population within Iraq's borders has created further instability, especially in the capital city of Baghdad, where nearly a quarter of the country's population resides. Interesting, though, is the comparative stability and prosperity of the people living in Iraqi Kurdistan, an autonomous region in the north of Iraq. Because they are largely isolated from the unrest between the Sunni and Shiites in the south and central parts of the country, as well as the fallout of the Iraq war, they have been able to enjoy stability and progress.

A proposed solution to struggles between Sunnis, Shiites, and **Kurds** in Iraq is to divide the country into three different parts for each group, but the distribution of oil reserves would clearly favor the Kurds and Shiites at Sunni expense, leaving the debate to rage on.

Resources, Commerce, and Trade

Iraq is unique among its Gulf region neighbors in that it boasts access to vast natural resources, both in fossil fuels and agriculture. Yet it lacks the port access its neighbors enjoy, making it difficult to export their wealth of crude oil.

Iraq's near landlocked position forces the country to ship their oil via pipelines to other countries' ports, across the land of its anxious neighbors. Surrounding Iraq are six countries still concerned with the outcome of a war started nearly fifteen years ago. This is both because many of these nations have, in the last twenty years, fought with or against Iraq for territorial and religious reasons and they stand to benefit or suffer from a change in Iraq's oil distribution or a redrawing of the countries' lines.

In 2014, 85 percent of Iraq's exports were crude oil, totaling 95 percent of their foreign-made income. That said, Iraq, unlike some of its desert neighbors, is still able to produce crops and raise livestock, and has a developed manufacturing industry. Agriculture and services account for 35 percent of their gross domestic product (GDP).

As security in the country improved from 2007 to 2013, the economy slowly evened out, with **inflation**—or lowered value of currency commonly seen in the increased price of goods—gradually decreasing over time to roughly 2 percent in 2013. Compared to the United States (which has experienced unusual inflation patterns since the 2008 recession, and even risks slipping into deflation) a consistent inflation rate of 2 percent is healthy and implies a strengthening economy. However, since 2013, a continued civil war and the rise of Sunni extremist group the Islamic State (IS) has led to increasing fears about the country's political, social, and economic security.

Kuwait

As with many of the countries in the Middle East, Kuwait has passed through many hands, starting with the Greeks in 2000 BCE, nomadic tribes in the 1700s (among whom were the al-Sabah family, who rule today), and the British, who took control of the country in 1899 to defend against Ottoman expansion. The nation finally gained independence in 1961. Neighboring Iraq has tried multiple times to gain control of Kuwait but has been repeatedly thwarted by international efforts.

Located at the northernmost tip of the Persian Gulf, Kuwait is dwarfed by its large neighbors, Iran, Iraq, and Saudi Arabia, but its location is key in its successes, as well as past unrest. It is a nation in transition, geographically, politically, and religiously. Essentially blocking Iraq from the Persian Gulf, Kuwait enjoys resources from the open sea as well as a wealth of oil.

Kuwait is in some ways a wealth of contradiction. The population alone tells an interesting story: of 4.2 million people, nearly 3 million are expatriates, while the remaining 1.2 million are Kuwaitis. The country is thought to enjoy greater freedom of the press than its Gulf region neighbors, yet the press is forbidden to speak out against God, religion, or the president. Even more astonishing is that Kuwaiti women only won the right to vote in 2005!

Resources, Commerce, and Trade

While some aspects of Kuwaiti life may seem volatile, the economy is strong in many ways. Their currency, the dinar, is the highest valued in the world, they have the fourth highest income per capita of any country, and their oil reserves are the sixth largest globally. These massive oil reserves were found in 1939, and for the next forty years, the country went through great waves of modernization.

Petroleum is the country's main export, accounting for 94 percent of export revenues. 56 percent of exports are in crude oil and 31 percent in refined products. Kuwait's service-based economy is supported by shipping, water-desalinization (removing the salt from sea water to make it potable), and banking. As early pioneers of diversifying away from a petroleum-based economy, Kuwait has developed internationally recognized financial systems and boasts some of the largest banks in the region. Unfortunately, recent political disputes have made meaningful economic reforms difficult, and little progress has been made since the Gulf War in 1990.

While this could be a source of frustration for Kuwaiti citizens, many have taken matters into their own hands, starting informal online businesses and utilizing platforms like Instagram to sell their wares.

Oman

The Sultanate of Oman is an absolute monarchy consisting of two major parts: the eastern portion of the Arabian Peninsula, and a small cape that juts out into the Persian Gulf. Though insignificant in landmass, this cape creates a narrow **choke point** for ships entering the gulf. Choke points, where a waterway narrows and causes ships to slow down and make sharp turns, can be dangerous both because they increase the probability of collision, but also because they make these ships targets for pirates and terrorist attacks.

This small Arab nation has a long history that makes it culturally and economically different from its neighbors. Between the 1700s and 1900s, Oman proved to be a powerful force, dominating trade in the area and vying with the United Kingdom for control in the Persian Gulf region. Though the country has oil reserves, they are modest, especially in comparison to neighboring Saudi Arabia and Qatar. The discovery of vast resources in these nearby countries led to Oman's diminished power. Yet, in 2010, the United Nations Development Program ranked Oman the most improved nation in the world for their development over the preceding forty years.

Resources, Commerce, and Trade

Oil exports are, on average, 5.5 billion barrels annually, making Oman the twenty-fifth largest exporter of oil in the world. But Oman's (comparatively) limited oil resources have encouraged the state to spend wisely, improving infrastructure for the population that lives and works there. They have also sought new sources of income, primarily in tourism, which is growing as more people are drawn to the country's large beaches and renovated ports. In fact, tourism is the country's fastest-growing industry, and the country has also invested in an international airport and luxury resorts to further attract foreign investment and business.

Because their oil revenues have been relatively low, especially compared with nearby Saudi Arabia and Qatar, Oman's citizens work at many different kinds of jobs. Even so, they have a multinational labor force, with nearly 50 percent of workers coming from outside of Oman. Most of these are from southern India and send their monthly earnings home—meaning vast sums of money are regularly leaving Oman's economy and entering that of other nations. Though these workers only make about $400 per month for agonizingly long days and difficult labor, the pay is still much better than in their home countries.

Qatar

Qatar, a bulbous peninsula extending off of Saudi Arabia into the Persian Gulf, has had a long, rich history of human inhabitants. Ancient tools have been found from early Stone Age people, dating back to fifty thousand years ago. Multiple empires ruled over this area, starting with the Mesopotamians around 10,000 BCE, and ending with the Ottoman Empire, which extended into Qatar as early as 1555 and ruled until 1915, when World War I began. In the midst of these many transitions, the area was introduced to Islam in 628 CE, when the Prophet Muhammad sent messengers to Munzir ibn Sawa al-Tamimi, a prominent Arab chief.

In 1916, Qatar signed a treaty with the British, promising not to cede any of their land to anyone but the British in exchange for their protection against foreign invaders—primarily Bahrain, an island nation in the Persian Gulf. This agreement with the British

Pearl farming is no longer the lucrative industry it once was, but some pearl farmers do still work along the Persian Gulf.

included provisions to end slavery, gunrunning, and piracy, and would last through the first and second World Wars.

When the treaties with Britain expired, the nine Arab states that shared in the treaty attempted to unite on their own. Unable to agree on terms, however, the states never joined, and Qatar declared independence on September 3, 1971.

Resources, Commerce, and Trade

In the eighth century, Qatar was an important center in the pearl trade. With a coastline that wraps around much of the country, Qatar was able to produce pearls, which provided a large national revenue. But the pearl trade in the Gulf region dried up in the 1940s, leaving the pearl trade as a distant legacy, a glimmer of heritage that is only referenced at patriotic events.

The discovery of oil and liquid natural gas in 1940 rapidly increased Western interest in the area. As World War II came to a close in 1944, Qatar was still in recovery from the collapse of the pearl trade, reduced food imports as a result of the World Wars, and the Great Depression in the 1930s. It wasn't until 1949 that Qatar began seeing revenues from their fossil fuels that led to spikes in immigration, wealth, and modernization.

Immigration to Qatar after the discovery of oil was so great that 90 percent of the population is made up of expatriates. This large divide between immigrants and nationals has a profound influence on the distribution of wealth.

Qatari nationals are given land and a monthly stipend for remaining in their home country, and the size of the stipend depends on how closely related one is to the ruling family. Because nationals are provided for, there's little incentive to work, though women will sometimes seek professional employment to escape arranged marriages and gain more autonomy from their families. This leaves many jobs, from construction worker to lawyer, in the hands of foreigners who are often paid based on nationality rather than merit.

Quality of Life

Though the region is rich with fossil fuels, it is a literal desert with little agricultural activity. Nearly all of the food in the country is imported and, as a result, it is incredibly expensive. Shipments can be lost, or left at port until all of the goods have spoiled. All of these complications further drive up the cost of food.

Fresh produce especially is sold at a premium, and because it has to travel so far to its destination, it often rots quickly. This also means a strong dependency on foreign goods. Neighboring Saudi Arabia is the primary provider of chicken. Whenever there is a dispute between the ruling families of Qatar and Saudi Arabia, there's no chicken at the store.

Lamb and goat meat come from Australia. Because Islam is the dominant religion in Qatar, most of the population eats **halal** food, which necessitates killing the animal right before eating. This means that live animals are shipped in poor conditions to Qatar's ports, where bureaucracy sometimes gets in the way of practicality.

For the Qatari nationals, Qatar is indeed a great place to live. Many luxuries are afforded this small group of residents as a result of the enormous revenues generated from natural gas. Even the professional, white-collar workers from other nations can enjoy a comfortable life. However, for hundreds of thousands of impoverished immigrants who build roads and resorts and live in squalor on the edges of cities, life is very difficult.

Saudi Arabia

One of the largest states in the Middle East, Saudi Arabia dominates the Gulf region with 830,000 square miles (2,149,690 sq. km) of desert, large oil reserves, and their claim as the birthplace of the prophet Muhammad. Saudi Arabia was originally divided into four regions. Ibn Saud, its founder and first monarch, began conquering and uniting the lands in 1901. He began with a territory known as Riyadh, which was his ancestral home. The Kingdom of Saudi Arabia wasn't officially founded until 1932.

Despite its size, Saudi Arabia is home to only 28.7 million people. Eight million of these inhabitants are expatriate workers who have come to take advantage of the prosperity of this oil-rich nation.

Resources, Commerce, and Trade

It is estimated that Saudi Arabia alone holds one quarter of the world's oil reserves. But with oil prices tied to a world market, revenue—and the social services that depend on them—can be unstable. The recent drop in oil prices has led Muhammed ibn Salman, the deputy crown prince of Saudi Arabia, to attempt to wean the country from its dependence on fossil fuels by 2020. His plan is to build tourism, manufacturing, and mining sectors, while tapping a resource that has gone ignored: women. Salman hopes that enticing more women to join the labor force will strengthen Saudi Arabia's economy.

Nearly 50 percent of Saudi Arabia's college graduates are women, and education is valued—but so are traditional values and gender roles. As Reuters reported after the new plan for the Saudi economy was released, "[These] changes ... would alter the social structure of the ultraconservative Muslim kingdom by pushing for women to have a bigger economic role and by offering improved status to resident expatriates."

As with many wealthy nations, the greatest percentage of wealth is enjoyed by the smallest percentage of citizens. While the country's largest cities continue to develop and modernize, traditional **Bedouin** nomads still travel ancient routes in search of scarce food and water for their livestock.

Not surprisingly, water is a limited and valuable resource in this large desert country. Though the Arab peninsula is surrounded by water, large parts of Saudi Arabia are removed from this resource. Even if the isolated central regions did have easier access to the waters of the Red Sea, Arabian Sea, Gulf of Adan, and Persian Gulf, the process of desalinization is expensive (and the water tastes terrible).

United Arab Emirates (UAE)

The United Arab Emirates (UAE) is a federation of seven **emirates**, or territories, wedged between Oman and Qatar. These seven territories include Abu Dhabi (which serves as the capital), Ajman, Dubai, Fujairah, Ras al-Khaimah, Sharjah, and Umm al-Quwain. Each emirate is a monarchy ruled by a single ruler called a **sheik**. These rulers combined make up the Supreme Council of Rulers, which presides over UAE governance.

Though the UAE has only been a nation, officially, since 1971, humans have inhabited the land for as many as 130,000 years. The discovery of stone tools suggests early migrants from Africa settled this region and over time began interacting with other cultures, such as the Mesopotamians.

Resources, Commerce, and Trade

The UAE shares elements of its economic history with neighboring Qatar. For instance, the pearling industry was historically the nation's largest asset, but it suffered after World War I and died out altogether with the introduction of the cultured pearl. The

The Burj Khalifa in Dubai is the tallest building in the world, adding to the modern city's prestige.

UAE and Qatar both gained independence in 1971 after the British military ended their protection treaties in the region. Also like Qatar, citizens of the UAE are paid for being nationals, and thus rarely work, instead hiring foreign laborers to fill a wide range of jobs. A telling indicator of this is the UAE's population demographics, which is made up of 1.4 million Emirati citizens and 7.8 million expatriate workers.

This collective nation is home to the elaborate city of Dubai, the top tourist destination in the Middle East—and the fifth most popular tourist destination in the world—as well as a growing financial center. Dubai is a city of unfettered opulence, boasting some of the most luxurious shopping malls in the world and the tallest structure in the world, the Burj Khalifa, which stands 2,700 feet (823 meters) high (roughly twice as tall as the Empire

State Building). The city will be home to the 2020 World Expo, a meeting of global innovators and thinkers who come together to showcase new technology and address global issues. This popularity and wealth is thanks in large part to the nation's enormous oil resources, the seventh largest in the world, and its huge natural gas resources, the seventeenth largest in the world.

Though Dubai is the most populous city in the UAE, Abu Dhabi is the capital and enjoys the highest oil production in the federation. Abu Dhabi is also an economic hub in the UAE, accounting for nearly 70 percent of the UAE's $400 billion economy. Abu Dhabi even tapped its impressive oil revenue streams to bail out Dubai in 2008, when the recession negatively impacted the real estate market and jobs in that growing city.

For Emirati citizens, life in the United Arab Emirates is indeed one of luxury. Unfortunately, that luxury is built on the labor of millions of foreigners. Though the Burj Khalifa is an impressive testament to the vast wealth of this relatively new nation, it, like so many other historic monuments of wealthy civilizations, is also a monument to the exploitation of millions of impoverished people.

Yemen

As recently as 1990, North Yemen and South Yemen joined to create what we know today as Yemen, which lies at the southern edge of the Arabian Peninsula, with Saudi Arabia to the north and Oman to the east. Large oil reserves have recently been discovered on Yemen's northern border with Saudi Arabia, and the country's position at the choke point on the Bab el Mandeb Strait, across

Brain Drain

Brain drain, or the migration of skilled and educated professionals, can exist anywhere and creates a domino effect throughout a country—or city's— economy and education. Even in the United States, we've seen the relocation of professionals from one city or state to another based on salaries, education, and how desirable one location is relative to another.

The places of origin lose the time and money spent educating these individuals, as well as these experts' contribution over the course of their lifetime. Brain drain presents other challenges, ranging from lacking skilled teachers and problem solvers who can help the nation keep pace with global advancements, to having a workforce incapable of rebuilding complicated industries in the wake of war and unrest.

Some argue that brain drain doesn't have to be inherently bad and that, in some cases, highly intelligent individuals leave their home countries to seek higher education and will return home as even greater assets. Though this is true in some cases, it has not been the case in Iraq or Iran. Throughout the War on Terror in Afghanistan and Iraq, skilled laborers left Iraq. Many were loyal citizens to their home country, but ultimately worried for the safety of their families and their own economic security and so migrated elsewhere.

from the Horn of Africa, gives it a strategic advantage. Because of these many recent changes and gains in resources, Yemen is one of the few countries on the Arabian Peninsula whose borders are still contested as neighbors and various populations within the country struggle for access to those recourses.

In 2011, citizens took to the streets to protest unemployment, government corruption, and rampant poverty. While these protests have led to regime change, they also opened the country to instability, which various **Islamist** groups have taken advantage of, further pressing Yemen into turmoil.

Resources, Commerce, and Trade

Yemen's economy has been challenged by an ongoing civil war, which began in 2015. The Heritage Foundation reports:

> *Numerical grading of Yemen's overall economic freedom has been suspended in the 2016 Index because of a significant deterioration in the quality of publicly available economic statistics on the country. Yemen's intensifying civil war has devastated the economy, destroying infrastructure, displacing over a million people, and creating an acute humanitarian crisis.*

As of 2013, Yemen was running a **deficit**, or debt, with national revenues around $7.7 billion and spending close to $12.3 billion. Exports included crude oil, coffee, and natural gas to China and Thailand, while imports were for machinery, foodstuffs, and chemicals mostly from the European Union and the United Arab Emirates.

Yemen enjoys relatively good agricultural land, and most Yemenis are employed in farming. Popular crops include barley and wheat, cotton, coffee, and fruits and vegetables. They also raise livestock, like sheep, goats, cattle, and camels. Khat, a mild narcotic that releases its stimulant when chewed, is also a popular crop in Yemen. So popular, in fact, that its production utilizes 40 percent of the nation's annual water from the Sana'a basin, leaving less water for produce and livestock, which in turn drives up the cost of food and pushes more of the population into poverty. This hike in food costs is associated with a nearly six percent rise in poverty in 2008 alone.

The Levant Region lies to the north and east of the Arabian Peninsula. Light green countries on this map are sometimes included in the Levant Region.

3

The Modern-Day Economy in the Levant Region

The Levant region of the Middle East includes Egypt in northern Africa, Jordan just across the Gulf of Aqaba, and Israel and Palestine wedged between them. Lebanon lies to the north of Israel, and Syria occupies a large portion of land north of Jordan.

Egypt

It is difficult to think of anything *but* history when one thinks of Egypt—pyramids, sphinxes, and hieroglyphics all come easily to mind. And indeed, Egypt has had a long, rich history.

Egypt has been populated since 40,000 BCE. It wasn't until much later, in 3150 BCE, that Upper and Lower Egypt unified and created what we think of as ancient Egyptian civilization. The Egyptians had a dynasty for nearly three millennia before being conquered by the Persian Empire around 600 BCE. The Persians were, in turn, conquered by Alexander the Great, for whom the Egyptian city Alexandria is named. Alexander the Great was a Macedonian ruler who conquered land from Greece to India; he came to Egypt in 332 and added it to his massive list of conquered nations. National uprisings against the new rule, however, led to a weak government, and Egypt was annexed and became a territory of Rome until 641 CE. Though Rome fell in 476 CE, parts of their vast realm continued to function with Constantinople (present-day Istanbul) in Turkey until the 600s.

In the 600s, Egypt was conquered by Islamic leaders and rotated under the rule of various caliphates. When Selim I, an Ottoman sultan, captured Cairo in 1517, Egypt joined the Ottoman Empire like so many other countries in the Middle East. In 1919, after World War I, Egypt was autonomous in theory, but Britain controlled military and foreign relations until 1954 when the present-day, modern Republic of Egypt was established.

Resources, Commerce, and Trade

Egypt has long prospered due to its proximity to the Nile River, which, for thousands of years, flooded its banks annually, watering crops and leaving behind nutrient-rich silt. On the northeastern coast of Africa, Egypt has enjoyed the bounty made possible by this resource, unlike the desert Gulf region, which struggles to produce most of its own food.

Farmers planned their crops around this annual flood until the construction of dams in the nineteenth century made it possible to store water and distribute it slowly, allowing farmers to grow food multiple times a year. As is often the case when humans attempt to control nature, this advancement has not been purely beneficial. Sitting water in the Aswan High Dam, which creates Lake Nasser in southern Egypt, has led to an increase in mosquitos carrying malaria and infecting residents. Adding pesticides to the water to address the insects has killed off many good insects that fish depend on for food, thus negatively impacting the fishing industry and a valuable source of protein for Egyptians. Finally, the irrigated water from the dam does not contain the same nutrient-rich silt that flood waters deposited seasonally, leaving the land infertile and necessitating the use of expensive chemical fertilizers which creates runoff that can negatively impact wildlife.

Egypt is also famous for its elaborate pyramids and artifacts. This rich cultural history has encouraged tourism for hundreds of years, bringing in revenues from other countries. This industry, however, is slowing down in the wake of increased Islamic extremism in the region.

Some oil resources have been found in the Western Desert region along the northwestern border with Libya, and in the Sinai region, a land bridge at the north end of the Red Sea connecting Egypt to Saudi Arabia. These deposits have helped Egypt remain self-sufficient despite the challenges their other industries face.

Jordan

Jordan's central location in the Levant means that it has been disproportionately affected by the disputes of its neighbors. When Israel became an independent nation in 1963, for example, Jordan gained two million Palestinian refugees from its new neighbor. More recently, as conflict in Syria escalates, Jordon has taken on 1.4 million Syrian refugees as well. This hospitality and tolerance is part of what makes Jordan one of the safest Arab states in the Middle East.

This diversity among Jordan's citizens is not new. Jordan was originally home to three separate ruling kingdoms in the third millennium BC. The Roman Empire and, later, the Ottoman Empire also moved through this area, creating a diverse cultural mix. In 1921, as the Ottoman Empire was dismantled by the European powers, the Emirate of Transjordan became one of many Middle Eastern British protectorates. The Hashemite Kingdom of Transjordan became a sovereign state in 1947. It became the Hashemite Kingdom of Jordan in 1948 after capturing the Gaza Strip from Israel (which was later lost in the Six-Day War).

But such generosity also comes at a price. Due to these ongoing struggles, Jordanians are now a minority in their own country, and the high number of refugees has strained its economy as well as other governmental systems.

Resources, Commerce, and Trade

Floods of refugees have had big impacts on Jordan's economy. Without oil reserves, the country has to rely on neighbors for energy and have only one remote port, limiting trade. There is very little water or farmable land in Jordan, so agriculture is of minimal benefit. Though Jordan has offered asylum to refugees fleeing from neighboring countries, they have also denied refugees the right to work for fear that native Jordanians will lose their jobs.

Despite these obstacles, Jordon has experienced relative prosperity. Jordan is considered an emerging **knowledge economy**, meaning the country has developed resources to compensate for its lack of natural resources. This includes manufacturing, technological, and chemical developments, and instituting a banking system that favors foreign investment. Jordan's industrial sector manufactures goods for cosmetics, textiles, pharmaceutical, defense, and aerospace businesses. It is this very reliance on knowledge that has offered Jordan relative stability despite the unrest in the region around them.

In the 1970s Jordan saw a massive, 350 percent increase in their gross domestic product, or GDP, per capita. The fluctuations over the next twenty years were relatively small. Since the present King, Abdullah II, took the throne in 1999, Jordan has seen a 7 percent annual growth in the economy. They have the third freest economy in the Middle East according to the Index of Economy Freedom and, in 2010, the KOF Index of Globalization declared Jordan the most globalized country in the Middle East and North Africa.

All in all, Jordan seems to be doing well despite its location in a turbulent region and lack of natural resources.

Lebanon

After the fall of the Ottoman Empire, French colonialists created the territory of Lebanon. In the 1930s, a mix of Christians and

In the 1930s Beirut, the capital of Lebanon, was bustling with tourists and new European residents.

Muslims populated the country. Their capital city, Beirut, was called the "Paris of the Middle East." In the late 1950s, however, Muslims outnumbered Christians and rebelled against the Christian-dominated government. The presence of Palestinian refugees caused further unrest, and the civil war that began in 1975 devastated the capital city and the Lebanese economy.

Neighboring Syria took control while the Iran-supported group, Hezbollah, found traction in Lebanon and even gained representation in its parliament. Hezbollah is a Shia militant group and political movement, and it has been classified as a terrorist organization by some countries, including the United States.

Lebanon was finally able to oust Syrian forces in 2005 with help from the United Nations. The UN placed a combined Sunni and Christian government in charge of reconstruction but, in 2006, Hezbollah and Israel rekindled previous aggression following the abduction of Israeli soldiers. Infrastructure was destroyed in the conflict, and Iran continues to fund Hezbollah in Lebanon today. Many Lebanese feel that so much outside influence blocks any chance of progress. Lebanon is home to many religious and ethnic factions, making religious and cultural disputes difficult to navigate, especially to an outsider.

Resources, Commerce, and Trade

Lebanon benefits from many natural resources, which include fossil fuels, agricultural land, and a long Mediterranean coastline that provides both ports for trade and resorts for tourism. Yet the economy still suffers as a result of perpetual conflict—sometimes from conflicts not even within Lebanon's own borders.

The civil war in Lebanon lasted until 1990 and nearly devastated the economy. It is thanks, in large part, to the window of peace that followed the war and the country's stable banking industry that it was able to experience growth. Soon after the conflict, the Lebanese government was able to begin collecting taxes, rebuild the capital city of Beirut, and attract tourists to its resorts.

A month-long war in 2006 nearly undid the years of rebuilding that had led to the country's relative stability. By focusing on real estate and tourism, Lebanon was able to rebuild its tourism sector, which saw enormous growth between 2008 and 2012 and accounted for roughly 10 percent of the national income. However, conflict has again gotten in the way of progress, this time in neighboring Syria. Tensions in Syria have led to a drop in tourism to Lebanon, as well as a flood of Syrian refugees entering the country, causing job shortages and a spike in poverty levels.

The Lebanese economic system is **laissez-faire**, meaning the government is uninvolved in private transactions and does not collect tariffs, enforce regulations, or offer subsidies. These policies further perpetuate high national debt, which was 130 percent of the country's GDP in 2015—down from 150 percent in 2010.

Israel

Israel was created from the British mandate of Palestine to create a home for the millions of nationless Jewish people living in the area in 1948. The Israeli-Arab conflict, which began following the creation of Israel, has dominated the region since the formation of this new country.

Following increased tensions in 1967, Israel and multiple Arab nations fought in what is known as the Six-Day War. The Arab nations experienced devastating losses, allowing Israel to claim even more land, including the Gaza Strip and the Sinai Peninsula from Egypt, the Golan Heights region from Syria, and the West Bank from Jordan. The Sinai Peninsula was eventually returned to Egypt, but the remaining tracts of land have been at the center of continued disputes between Israel and Arab nations ever since.

Resources, Commerce, and Trade

The Mediterranean Sea makes up the western border of Israel with Lebanon to the north, Syria to the northeast, Jordan and the West Bank to the east, and Egypt and the Gaza Strip to the southwest.

This location has long been contested, especially by Arab nations and displaced Palestinians, and it has a host of natural advantages.

Israel's location on the Mediterranean, for instance, provides the country with ports for importing and exporting goods. The oldest and largest of these is Haifa Port, but the country has added a new deepwater port, Ashdod, which allows heavy cargo ships to come into port and has increased trade.

In addition to important access to waterways, Israel boasts a highly educated population, allowing leading innovations in science and technology. Though bordered by a body of water, the country has experienced a shortage of clean water for drinking and agriculture. As need is often the mother of invention, Israel is leading the way in water technology, ranging from desalinization to recycling water. This has allowed Israel to remain fairly self-sufficient in terms of

Dan Shechtman, an Israeli professor, won the Nobel Peace Prize in Chemistry in 2011.

food, though it continues to import grains and meat. Other imports include military equipment, consumer goods, and rough diamonds. Interestingly, leading exports from Israel include cut diamonds, military technology, fruit, and chemicals.

As evidence of this small nation's large contribution to the sciences, six Israeli scientists have won the Nobel Prize in Chemistry in under ten years. Israel's universities for mathematics and the sciences are among the best in the world, and the country's second-largest city, Tel Aviv, is a modern, bustling hub of activity and technological advancement. The country has earned top rankings for their banking industry, economic stability in the face of crisis, and skilled manpower. Suffice it to say that growth and development in Israel is not just significant to the region, but to the whole world.

Palestine

The price of creating a new country for the persecuted Jewish population was displacing roughly eight million Palestinians who now lack a country of their own. Due to government-enforced exclusions and high levels of poverty, the Arab Palestinians have not been able to integrate with their Jewish neighbors. Thousands continue to live in impoverished refugee camps in continually shrinking territories within Israel's borders.

When Israel was established in 1948, the territories allocated for the Palestinians were the West Bank (including East Jerusalem) and the Gaza Strip. The historically and religiously significant city of Jerusalem provides a vivid illustration of the conflict between

Handcrafted Business in the Digital Age

Tel Aviv, Israel, is home to skilled artisans, trained in traditional crafts such as textiles, leather goods, and jewelry, some of whom have had success as international entrepreneurs by using websites like Etsy.com to sell their wares. The 2012 Etsy Seller's Survey found that 97 percent of Etsy shop owners operate their businesses from home, and 61 percent want their stores to stay independent and self-run. Perhaps unsurprisingly, 88 percent of Israeli Etsy shop owners are women, even though only 13 percent of businesses in Israel are woman-owned.

In a culture where women are traditionally less educated and less employable than men, technology has created an opportunity for women to gain financial independence. Candida Brush, a quantitative social researcher with Wellesley College, suggests, "because of [gendered] differential opportunity structures for employment in salaried jobs, turning to self-employment could be a means for women to overcome these structural barriers."

In an article posted on the Etsy blog about Israeli artists who use the site, Osnat Zilbershtein, the owner of the jewelry shop Omiya, says, "I think the fact that Etsy allows creative people here to work from their homes, and sell the things they are good at, [allows] artists to turn unfulfilled dreams into actual businesses."

these two nations. Because Jerusalem is an important city to Muslims, Jews, and Christians alike, it has changed hands many times as religious leaders from different faiths lay claim to that land.

The BBC reports:

> More than 40 years ago, Israel's army captured East Jerusalem from Jordan in the June 1967 War. The area fell in the heat of a deadly battle, but Israel did not massacre its Palestinian inhabitants or destroy its holy shrines like the medieval Christian knights. From the Jewish perspective 1967 brought the "reunification" of the holy city, restoring a divine plan after centuries of interruption.

Palestinian citizens in the West Bank area of East Jerusalem are today forced to lead complicated double lives. Though they live there, they must acquire Israeli residency permits, which are increasingly difficult to get. Often their own building and development projects suffer at the hands of Israel's bureaucracy, limiting Palestine's growth. Palestinians find it difficult to get jobs and experience the higher quality of life they see their Israeli neighbors enjoy.

But the conflict is more complicated than evil Israelis persecuting their Palestinian countrymen. In "What the Media Gets Wrong About Israel," an article written by Matti Friedman for *The Atlantic*, she explains that this simplistic narrative is partially the result of international journalists in a foreign country trying to learn the nuances of a complicated conflict and depending on one another for information. Also, editors often "kill" stories that

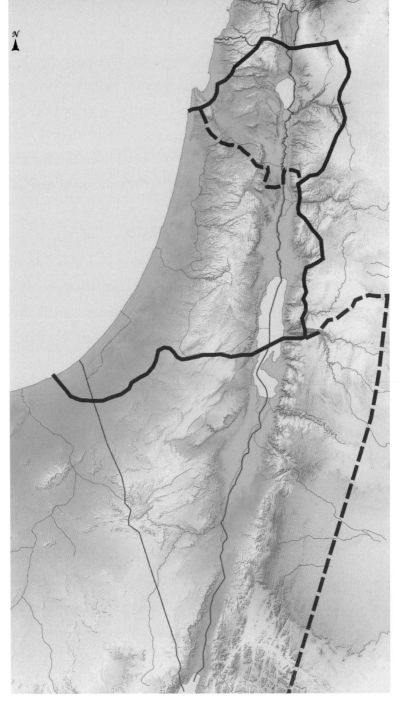

Since Israel became its own country in 1948, Palestinians have gradually lost a territory of their own and have been allocated an ever-shrinking portion of the country. These red and green lines indicate larger historical boundaries.

contradict established narratives the paper is following both for consistency and for safety. For instance, Israel's aggressive behavior toward Palestinians is portrayed by certain newspapers as bullying, yet instances of Palestinian suicide bombings, Hamas threats, and militant rallies might not be reported by the same newspapers.

Resources, Commerce, and Trade

How does one measure the economic well-being of a nation without internationally recognized, defined borders? Upon what resources and services is the economy built? While these are complicated questions to answer definitively, there are some answers that sketch a rough picture of Palestine's state of affairs.

The territories belonging to Palestine depend heavily on agriculture for jobs and income. Official reports suggest that agriculture employs roughly 13 percent of the working population, but it is estimated that the real number is much higher, with some estimates as high as 90 percent. This discrepancy is the result of unreported income or working "under the table," which is often the case so larger companies can avoid paying taxes and pay their employees below minimum wage. Employees, on the other hand, are willing to take these low-paying jobs because there are few alternatives for making money when Israeli bureaucracy blocks many other jobs for Palestinians. Olives are the territory's main crop and account for a large portion of exports as well, though this key means of national income is hampered by minimal access to ports. Additionally, it is estimated that the Israeli government has uprooted 800,000 olive trees since the Six-Day War in 1967, further limited Palestinian economic well-being.

Because many Palestinians struggle to find work in the Gaza Strip, with unemployment booming at nearing 25 percent, this population often, ironically, looks to Israel for employment. The only available jobs for Palestinians in Israel are often low-paying and dangerous construction and manufacturing jobs. These positions come with little job security and high exposure to toxic materials and poor working conditions.

With such a diffuse economy comes the opportunity for corruption. The *Guardian* reports that instances of corruption are frequent and wide-ranging in Palestine, from pharmaceutical companies distributing expired food and medication to tax evasion.

All of these factors play into the complicated economic situation in the area. But the conflict remains in the Palestinians' ardent fight to protect their culture and religion. These cultural elements also play a role in the economy, as religious tourists travel to the region on spiritual journeys and the native people create traditional crafts to sell. This is a region that the entire world is watching, with hopes of a resolution.

Syria

Interestingly, the word Syria was originally synonymous with Levant and referred to the entire region. Today, however, Syria refers to 71,000 square miles (183,889 sq. km) to the south of Turkey, west of Iraq, and north of Jordan and Israel. The northern half of Syria's western border touches the Mediterranean Sea while the southern half borders Lebanon.

Syria is home to the oldest continuously inhabited city in the world, Damascus. You may recognize the city from the Christian Bible as the city where the Apostle Paul was baptized, or as the site of the Umayyad Mosque, one of the oldest mosques in the world. Religion still plays a vital role in the lives of Syrians. Though 75 percent of the country's population is Sunni Muslim, the Shiite minority has aggressively maintained control over the government for decades.

As with many of the Middle Eastern countries, Ottomans ruled in Syria until the First World War, when the Middle East was divided between France and Britain. It was not until 1945 that Syria gained independence from France and became a founding member of the United Nations.

From the beginning of its independence until 1970, Syria suffered a string of conflicts and coups that lead to a volatile government and economy. In 1970, Hafez al-Assad became president and ruled until 2000, when his son, Bashar al-Assad, took over as president. Since 2011, when the Arab Spring spread across the Middle East, a civil war has devastated the country.

Syria has been in the news in recent years because waves of refugees are fleeing the violence and instability of the government to neighboring countries as well as more distant European nations, some of which are more welcoming than others.

Resources, Commerce, and Trade

As a result of ongoing civil war, the Syrian economy is part state-owned, in which businesses are run on behalf of the government, and part war economy. Philippe Le Billion describes a war economy

Old Damascus, a city of great religious import to many denominations, is the oldest city in the world.

as a "system of producing, mobilizing and allocating resources to sustain the violence." This is accomplished by raising taxes and reallocating resources for military purposes.

Syria's resources include oil and agriculture. Though commercial levels of oil were found in 1956, Syria has since become a net importer of oil as production has been in free fall since 2011. With over four million Syrian citizens fleeing the turmoil, tax revenues have declined as well. Heavy state involvement in business has further slowed economic progress, and the ongoing conflict has deterred international investment. This paints a bleak picture for the future and those that still live there.

One of the reasons the Middle East is an imperfect moniker is that the region extends all the way to the Western edge of Africa, just south of Spain.

4

The Modern-Day Economy in North Africa

orth Africa is the northernmost region of the African continent, which has experienced much cultural exchange from both European countries and Arab nations. The region is typically defined as including Algeria, Libya, Morocco, and Tunisia. Oftentimes, these countries are referred to as the Magreb, which is the Arabic word for "sunset."

Algeria

Algeria, once occupied by France, has struggled to prosper since its declaration of independence on July 5, 1962. Despite the devastating war it took to liberate them from the French, more Algerians live in France today than in their own capital city of Algiers.

The rise of Islam has also caused tensions in Algeria, where a conflict between the existing regime and those seeking to make the country an Islamic republic resulted in massive bloodshed. After a resolution was met in 2005, wherein the government granted amnesty to those who sought to overthrow it, new contentions arose with indigenous North Africans called Berbers who resented their lack of representation in the new Algerian government. Berbers were once the dominant ethnicity in Algeria, but were gradually Arabized over time, so while many are Berber descendants, they also identify as Arab.

Resources, Commerce, and Trade

Since it gained independence in the 1960s, Algeria has had a history of socialist economics, leaving much of the nation's financial power and development in the hands of the government. Unfortunately, this has led to little innovation in industry outside of hydrocarbons, or mining. As with many of the oil-rich countries of the Middle East, the Algerian hydrocarbon industry has been a strong source of income despite its volatility. Because oil prices are fixed to a world market, the prices dropped from overproduction in the 1980s and led to a temporary economic downturn in the country.

It is precisely this volatility that has encouraged Algerians to invest in other types of industry. Agriculture, for instance, has become an important part of the Algerian economy. Nearly 14 percent of the population is employed in agriculture and,

Olive trees, like those pictured above, are a staple of the Algerian agricultural industry.

between 2010 and 2011, the country saw a 10 percent growth in this field.

In 2006, Vladimir Putin, President of Russia, visited Algeria and forgave $4.7 billion of Soviet-era debt. To show his gratitude, Algerian President Abdelaziz Bouteflika purchased $7.5 billion worth of arms and military planes from Russia. After protests for economic reform at the beginning of 2011, the government implemented retroactive raises and public grants totaling $23 billion. In the last five years, public spending has increased by 27 percent, which has helped to grow the economy.

Libya

For centuries, Libya was ruled by invading nations. First the Phoenicians, then Greeks, Romans, Arabs (who brought with them Islam), the Ottomans, and Italians took control of this North African country. In 1942, British and French forces split Libya, and finally, in 1951, Libya declared independence.

In 1969, Colonel Muammar Qaddafi, inspired by Egyptian President Gamal Abdel Nasser's revolutionary activity a decade earlier, deposed Libya's king and became dictator at the tender age of twenty-seven. Though the king had supported modernizing and the nation's constitution, quality of life in Libya was abysmally low. Citizens were frustrated by low literacy rates (at a troubling 10 percent), poor housing options, and a short life expectancy of only fifty-seven years. Furthermore, the Libyan population saw the king as being too influenced by Western interests.

Qaddafi, on the other hand, was adamantly opposed to imperialist influence and gained support with his pro-Arab, pro-African ideology. Internationally, he was less popular, as many countries worried about his human rights violations, including silencing the press, and disappearances, torture, and terrorism. Qaddafi is famous for having grown increasingly eccentric over the course of his forty-year reign, until he was ousted and killed in the 2011 Libyan civil war.

On July 7, 2012, the nation saw its first free election in forty years. This event was made even more remarkable as almost thirty women were elected into parliament. Unfortunately, continued civil unrest has led to increased instability since then.

Resources, Commerce, and Trade

Though he was a controversial figure, many positive changes occurred during Qaddafi's leadership. Literacy rates soared to

90 percent, and welfare systems were put in place to assist with education, housing, and health care. While some heralded Qaddafi as a great leader, he made many enemies on the international stage. These conflicts have complicated Libya's current economic situation, leading to UN-supported economic sanctions and warring militias claiming ownership of oil.

The Heritage Foundation, a conservative research think tank based in Washington, DC, has reported that the political instability in Libya makes information about the economy unreliable, and corruption further obscures the real economic situation. Taxes, which are relatively low at a maximum of 10 percent for individuals and 20 percent for businesses, are not effectively enforced because the current government is at odds within its own ranks. This has trickled down to the population who suffer the resulting high unemployment rates. Since hydrocarbons account for 95 percent of the nation's income, a global drop in oil prices has translated to lower wages and heightened disputes over who is, in fact, in control of the oil resources.

As the African Economic Outlook (AEO) states in their report on Libya, "Post-2011 Libya has ... witnessed the rise of geographical, tribal and ethnic tensions. A resolution to such disparities and a process of national dialogue would be key elements of a successful political and economic transition."

Morocco

Morocco, just across the Sea of Gibraltar from Spain, is greatly influenced by its position between Africa and Europe, even while certain aspects of its culture are conservative and traditional. Though a fraction of the landmass of other Middle Eastern countries, such as neighboring Algeria, Morocco boasts roughly the same population: 32.7 million.

Evidence suggests that Morocco has been inhabited since Paleolithic times, as long as 210,000 years ago. In the sixth century BCE, the Phoenicians established colonies in the area as well as important trading routes. These settlements were lost to the Carthaginians and again changed hands in the first century BCE when the Romans took over the region. As the Roman Empire collapsed, new invading groups entered the area, including the Vandals and Visigoths.

Morocco continued to change hands and gain diverse influences, including the arrival of Islam in 670. By the 1800s, Europe had industrialized and looked across the Mediterranean at Africa for colonization. French colonists bought up fertile farmland in Morocco, and the French government welcomed this protective barrier between itself and Algeria.

As other competing European powers vied for a piece of Moroccan territory, tensions increased between them. France asserted dominance over the culture, which angered many Moroccans, although some French leaders worked toward a joint government. However, there were also many shared goals between the French and Algerians. During both World Wars, Moroccan military personnel fought with the French military. As the World Wars came to an end, however, nationalist movements for independence led the French to take a more militant stand against the native people, driving a wedge of hostility between them.

After the French exiled the popular Sultan Muhammad V in 1953, the movement for independence redoubled its efforts and began resorting to violence. The French protectorate in Morocco ended, and other European powers withdrew from the country.

In 1961, King Hassan II took over as king. His reign is associated with numerous human rights violations and a need for political reforms. Upon King Hassan II's death in 1999, his son, King Mohammed VI, ascended to the throne and began to address the needed reforms in both the country's economy and its social life. While these moves toward change appeased citizens for a time, terrorist attacks have left the nation feeling unsettled, and many protested the government during the Arab Spring in 2011, demanding limits be placed on the king's power.

Resources, Commerce, and Trade

Morocco's economy has made gains toward joining the world market. This is in part because the country has been key in the United States's fight against Islamic terrorism. The government's increased efficiency and relative moderation have invited foreign investment, tourism, and improved civil liberties for residents.

The staples of Morocco's economy include agriculture, phosphates, and tourism. Agriculture makes up 14 percent of the economy and employs over 40 percent of the population. The production of phosphates, often used in fertilizers and livestock feed, also helps support this dominant industry. Unfortunately, irrigation is unreliable, though there have been deliberate attempts to improve accessibility to water.

Morocco's natural biodiversity, interesting landscapes, and long, rich cultural history have intrigued people from all over the world, leading to a strong tourism industry. The country's goal is to double the number of visitors it had in 2010 by 2020. If they achieve this goal, tourism would account for 20 percent of the nation's GDP. The banking sector is beginning to establish itself in the region and plays an ever-increasing role in the economic well-being of the country.

As the economy improves and Morocco becomes increasingly modernized, quality of life for its citizens will also improve. Joining the world market and inviting tourists may also help pave the way for improved civil liberties.

Tunisia

Tunisia has had a long and varied history. First occupied by Berbers, the country was later controlled by Carthaginians and then by the Romans. In the 1500s, the Ottoman Empire seized this North African state, and remained in power until 1881, when the French invaded. It wasn't until Habib ibn Ali Bourguiba, a young lawyer, led a movement for independence in 1934, that the nation began its path to autonomy. In 1957, Habib Bourguiba became the country's first president; he remained in power until 1987. As with all leaders, Bourguiba had an agenda, and he immediately set about modernizing his country by improving education, reforming gender inequality, and negotiating strong foreign relationships.

Resources, Commerce, and Trade

Though the smallest nation in North Africa, Tunisia enjoys a higher gross national income (GNI) than its neighbors, as well as relative political stability, lots of fertile land, and efficient use of its limited fossil fuels. Tunisia also has stronger relationships with European countries and the EU, which have continued to improve as the Tunisian government becomes increasingly progressive.

In addition to agriculture, Tunisia makes roughly 25 percent of its national income from industry. They manufacture shoes, clothes, car parts, and machinery. The country's strong foreign relationships have also helped them export the many goods they manufacture; the European Union accounts for 75 percent of their exports.

These many benefits have also improved quality of life for Tunisians. Citizens of Tunisia have longer life expectancies, higher incomes, and higher levels of education (on average) than do other North African countries.

As evidence of the nation's modernity, the capital city of Tunis has approved a five million dollar building project called Tunis Sports City. This mini city will be built in the capital's northern suburbs and includes eleven high-rise apartments, fifty houses, and thirteen blocks of apartments and townhomes. Sports City differs from other building developments in that it caters specifically to athletic residents, with athletic academies for a variety of sports, a football stadium, and a swimming center with an Olympic-sized pool, as well as a sports rehabilitation facility.

Where are the Women?

While the most famous examples of leadership across the Middle East tend to be men, women have played a vital role in the development, modernization, and economic well being of their nations.

In "Leadership in the Middle East: Women in Lebanon," an article co-written by Judith Cochran, Mona Nabhani, Rima Bahous, and Rewa Zeinati, the authors claim that many ambitious and educated women are influencing the policies in the Middle East but are hidden behind an impenetrable wall of men. Many of the countries in the Middle East have only allowed women to vote in the last decade—shockingly recent when compared with women's movements in other regions. The female leaders interviewed pointed out that this gender divide is ingrained in the culture and religion of Lebanon and other countries, ultimately affecting their nation's politics and economy. Because men have written the laws in place for the benefit of men, and women have long been stopped from weighing in, half the population has no voice in the values and development of their countries.

As is often the case, this divide is rooted in education. Only wealthy women in the region can afford an education, and because girls are often married off to other families, educating a daughter is seen as "tending to someone else's garden." An unnamed interviewee in the article stated:

> Education is empowerment on the personal and social levels. Educated women have more self-confidence and higher self-esteem. Also, educated women get better jobs and have a higher chance of becoming financially independent, which increases their ability to make the best decisions for their lives, such as leaving a bad marriage or seeking higher degrees.

Perhaps an unexplored solution to unemployment, lack of diversification in industry, and poverty is to educate women of all backgrounds and empower them to take on leadership roles. Such an initiative would bring the other half of the population in countries like Lebanon into the economy and have wide-reaching effects for everyone.

Muammar Qaddafi, former leader of Libya

5

Important Figures in the Economy across the Middle East

Across the Middle East, key figures have helped shape the culture and economy of the region. From militant leaders like Muammar Qaddafi, to the man who inspired him, President Gamal Abdel Nasser, many powerful people have had a profound impact on the values and progress of the countries of this region, and, in turn, affected its economies.

The Gulf Region

Sheikha Lubna al-Qasimi

As the current minister of international cooperation and development, former minister of foreign trade, and minister of the economy before that, Sheikha Lubna al-Qasimi is the first woman to hold any ministerial post in the United Arab Emirates.

After completing an undergraduate degree in Computer Science at California State University, Chico, al-Qasimi returned to the UAE to take a position in Dubai as a program developer in 1981. She was later put in charge of automating all of the information for the UAE's federal government. Her career had other exciting responsibilities in store as well, including a position as senior manager of information systems at the largest port in the Middle East, Dubai Ports Authority. She held this position for seven years and, in 1999, was recognized by the ruler of Dubai with the Distinguished Government Employee Award. Her later work developing e-commerce with Tejari, the first business-to-business marketplace in the Middle East, won that company a World Summit award in 2003.

In 2004, al-Qasimi became minister of the economy and seems never to have looked back. Each post this powerful woman takes on has led her to have greater influence over the people who live in her country. In 2008, she was appointed minister of foreign trade, and she began her current position as minister of international cooperation and development in 2013. But she has also taken on a host of other responsibilities including President of Zayed University and head of the UAE Committee of Humanitarian Aid.

Minister for Foreign Trade, Sheikha Lubna al-Qasimi, is a leader in the United Arab Emirates and has advanced quickly through the ranks in her field since the 1990s.

In 2015, *Forbes* magazine ranked Sheikha Lubna al-Qasimi as one of the most powerful women in the world and commended her **philanthropic**, or charitable, commitments. Under her leadership, the UAE increased charitable donations from 1.6 billion to 5.4 billion. Al-Qasimi also donates her time to the Friends of Cancer Patients Society and the Dubai Autism Center.

The Levant Region

King Abdullah II of Jordan

King Abdullah II is named for his great grandfather, who founded Jordan, and has been in power since ascending to the throne in February of 1999. A member of the Hashemite family, which has ruled Jordan since it broke from the Ottoman Empire in 1921, he is considered a descendant of the Prophet Muhammad—an important characteristic for a ruler in an Islamic country. In 2016, Abdullah II was voted the most influential Muslim in the world by *The Muslim 500* magazine. He was awarded this distinction for his significant role in two of the major conflicts currently affecting the Middle East: the conflict in Syria and the Palestinian/Israeli conflict.

Since becoming king in 1999, King Abdullah II has set up special economic zones, improved relationships between the public and private sectors, and established a free-trade agreement with the United States. These efforts have resulted in an improved economy and increased foreign investment. Economic growth has doubled under the king's leadership, from 3 to 6 percent annually, and encouraged other Western countries as well as Gulf nations to

King Abdullah II of Jordan and his wife, Queen Rania, have worked tirelessly to improve quality of life in Jordan.

invest directly in Jordan. The king has also installed programs for alternative energy systems, like solar power, which simultaneously diversify the economy and are estimated to reduce carbon dioxide emissions by 352,739,619 pounds (160,000,000 kilograms) a year. Information and communication technology programs have also been made a staple of Jordanian education, making the country's telecommunications sector one of the strongest in the region

The economy has also flourished because Jordan enjoys greater stability and safety than do many of its neighbors. The nation's ability to play a role in ameliorating conflicts around it and offering tolerance to many different groups of people increases international trust and improves crosscultural exchange. In 2008, the king began a campaign called "Decent Housing for Decent Living," which guarantees all Jordanians and refugees housing and access to health care and education.

While traveling in 2005, King Abdullah II met with Pope Benedict XVI to maintain a relationship that had been initiated with Pope John Paul II and to consider new ways to encourage peace between Muslims and Christians. Later in the year, he spoke to the Catholic University of America's Columbus School of Law in service of these objectives of peace. King Abdullah II released Toujan al-Faisal, Jordan's first female member of parliament and an outspoken supporter of free speech, after she was jailed for slandering the government. He has also issued a decree forbidding the detention of journalists in Jordan and has made women's rights an important issue during his leadership.

The Muslim 500 quotes King Abdullah II as saying, "The fact is, humanity is bound together, not only by mutual interests, but by shared commandments to love God and neighbor."

North Africa

Habib Ben Ali Bourguiba

Though Habib Ben Ali Bourguiba eventually traveled to France for his education in law and French literature, he was born to a modest family in Tunisia. The youngest of eight children, it was

A leader in Tunisia's fight for independence and a champion of women's rights, President Habib Bourguiba nevertheless fell from favor toward the end of his political career.

thanks to an older brother's generosity that Bourguiba was able to study abroad at all. And it was a good thing he did.

Bourguiba led the country to independence from French rule in 1956 upon returning to his home country. The education he'd received in France was not just scholastic—he also saw women who were free to go to work or marry whomever they chose. In Paris, Bourguiba also saw many people of different beliefs living together in peace. These were the ideals he brought back to his own country along with a commitment to education and moderate policies.

When Bourguiba passed away at age ninety-six in 2000, a *New York Times* obituary written by Eric Pace described his contributions to Tunisian women in particular:

> *Mr. Bourguiba used his power to achieve a major gain for women. He pushed through a "code of personal status" that ran counter to traditional Muslim jurisprudence and custom in enhancing women's rights.*
>
> *Polygamy was outlawed. Marriage was redefined as a voluntary contract that conferred rights upon the wife as well as the husband. A minimum age for marriage was established, and the consent of the bride was made mandatory. These stipulations in effect outlawed the traditional practice of selling young girls. They also underscored the modern concept of marriage as a bond between individuals rather than an alliance between families.*

These social ideals had economic consequences. Initially, Bourguiba sought to establish socialist economic policies, but when this didn't work, he returned to the drawing board. He worked closely with his Prime Minister, Hedi Nouira, on a new plan that was economically liberal and pro-Western. This encouraged private business within Tunisia as well as trade and commerce with other nations, especially those in Europe.

Though Bourguiba profoundly affected the future of his homeland with his forward-thinking ideology, his story is not without dark moments. After returning to Tunisia from France, Bourguiba married his second wife, Wassila ben Ammar, who was politically active and advocated for a democratic society. She also worked toward a peaceful transition when her husband was ousted from his role as president in 1986 by his new prime minister, Zine el-Abidine Ben Ali. The new prime minister declared Bourguiba, who was then eighty-four years old, too senile to run the country. Among the indications that this was true was that Bourguiba reportedly appointed officials to new posts and then later claimed to have never done so. The former president also decided to banish ben Ammar and divorce her, presumably for her insistence on a democratic government, which would have called his absolute authority into question.

Bourguiba's decline toward the end of his presidency, as the *New York Times* reports, led to a host of economic woes. According to Pace, "In the last years of the Bourguiba era, Tunisia was racked by economic problems and discontent, underscored by bread riots in 1984. Unemployment was painfully high, particularly among the young."

Even so, Bourguiba's early contributions set Tunisia on a path toward being one of the most economically and politically stable nations in the Arab world.

Gamal Abdel Nasser

Gamal Abdel Nasser is one of the most illustrious figures in the Middle East's recent history. Born in Alexandria in 1918 to a postal worker and a supportive mother, he worked his way up through Egypt's military ranks to take on the colonial forces controlling his country.

Nasser's first opportunity at a life in politics was his involvement in a protest against British manipulation of the Egyptian royal family when he was just fifteen years old. Nasser graduated from the Royal Academy in 1938 and joined the Egyptian military, where he continued to speak out against British colonialism. As Britain tightened its grasp on its territories in Africa and the Middle East, Nasser became increasingly intolerant of the imposition. He used his position as an instructor in the Egyptian Army Staff College to share his views with other young officers who were more likely to be moved by his impassioned lessons than older officers.

The 1947 war against Israel further spurred Nasser to action. The Egyptian army was outfitted with faulty weapons for the conflict, and many believed it was the result of a scandal involving the Egyptian royal family. Nasser used this as a chance to band together with his fellow Egyptian soldiers who felt the entire system of government needed to change.

Gamal Abdel Nasser is a much-beloved figure in Egypt's history. Leader of Egypt's liberation movement, Nasser gave voice to widespread frustration of the Arab world, seeking political and economic independence from Western powers.

It wasn't until five years later, though, that Nasser led a revolt against the royal family. Believing that the public would not support such as young officer of low rank, Nasser asked General Muhammad Neguib to lead the revolt as a figure head, or representative leader.

Nasser's Republic, The Making of Modern Egypt

Beginning in 2011, before the uprisings in Egypt, documentary filmmaker Michal Goldman released the first documentary made for an American audience about the life—and lasting effects—of President Gamal Abdel Nasser.

The director, a Boston native, was praised by the Boston Globe for providing meaningful historical context about an historical figure who has had a profound impact on the world but is woefully unknown in the Western world. The Boston Globe reviewer, Peter Keough, wrote, "Goldman demonstrates Gamal Abdel Nasser ... was committed to promoting Arab progress, African liberation, and an end to Western colonialism. But [by] becoming Egypt's first military dictator, [he set] a precedent that has plagued the country ever since."

The film is driven by the voices of modern Egyptians who are still debating their history and identity as they face yet another volatile period, one that harkens back to Nasser's own time in power. The filmmaker herself describes Nasser as, "A man of enormous charisma and ambition, [who] began a revolution he could not complete."

While the Egyptian public was willing to support the revolt as well as General Neguib as its leader, there was trouble within the movement. Neguib was elected the first president of Egypt with Nasser as his right-hand man, but Neguib distanced himself from the movement's ideology and aligned himself with the Muslim Brotherhood, a political party. In late 1954, an independent member of the Muslim Brotherhood attempted to assassinate Nasser as he gave a speech in Alexandria. As the crowd erupted into chaos, eight shots rang out, but none hit Nasser, whose speech was broadcast throughout the Arab world via radio. He urged the crowd to remain calm, saying:

> My countrymen, my blood spills for you and for Egypt. I will live for your sake and die for the sake of your freedom and honor. Let them kill me; it does not concern me so long as I have instilled pride, honor, and freedom in you. If Gamal Abdel Nasser should die, each of you shall be Gamal Abdel Nasser ... Gamal Abdel Nasser is of you and from you and he is willing to sacrifice his life for the nation.

This speech solidified his popularity in Egypt and throughout the Arab world, and he became the second president in 1955 after Neguib was put on house arrest.

Nasser's primary objective as president was to remove British influence over Egypt and the Suez Canal. In 1957, as Nasser further shaped the new government, he prioritized women's suffrage, or right to vote, and prohibited gender-based discrimination, including protection for women in the workplace.

To address the need for more irrigable land and energy recourses, Nasser proposed the building of the Nasser Dam. This effort was originally to be funded by the United States and Britain, despite the rough history between Egypt and Britain. However, in the wake of other international alliances between Egypt, China, and the Soviet Union, both the United States and Britain revoked their support. In order to fund the dam, Nasser announced the nationalization of the Suez Canal. This led swiftly to the Suez Conflict, in which France, Britain, and Israel, fearful of losing control of this important conduit for the shipment of oil, joined forces to overtake the Sinai Peninsula and the Suez Canal city of Port Said.

Despite their own objections to Egypt's involvement with China and the Soviet Union, US President Dwight D. Eisenhower and his administration worked with the UN to put a stop to the invasion. Both the French and British troops withdrew from the canal zone one week later, although the Sinai was under Israeli occupation until March 1957.

Conflict between Israel and Egypt continued, however. In May 1967, Israel attacked the Egyptian air force and the Six-Day War began. Crushing defeat followed crushing defeat until Israel claimed the Sinai and the Gaza Strip from Egypt, the West Bank from Jordan, and the Golan Heights from Syria. Nasser was so humiliated by this massive military failure that he resigned from office. Across Egypt and other Arab nations his supporters took to the street, protesting his resignation. Bolstered by this outpouring of support, Nasser retook office.

In his final years as president, Nasser made explicit moves toward a more liberal and democratic government and focused on foreign relationships. In 1970, however, Nasser died of a heart attack after meeting with several Arab leaders. He had been suffering from a host of health complications, which were unknown to the public until his death, and had even had two heart attacks prior to this fatal event in 1970.

Nasser's legacy lives on. His many progressive policies and ideas for independence, Arab nationalism, and civilian leadership helped to bolster Egypt's floundering economic and political systems, establishing the country as an important force in world events.

Chronology

200 BCE   Early banking systems are established along trade routes in the Middle East.

610–1258   Muslim conquests across Asia and Europe spread Islam.

1099   The Crusades begin, bringing Christian and Muslim populations in contact.

1299   The Ottoman Empire is founded by Osman I.

1908   Significant oil deposits are discovered in the Middle East.

1914–1919   World War I; fighting takes place in the Middle East, and Middle Eastern territories are redistributed among European powers.

1939–1945   World War II; independence movements begin across the Middle East.

1971   The British protectorate expires in the Gulf.

1956   Gamal Abdel Nasser becomes president of Egypt.

1967   The Six-Day War begins.

1990	Iraq invades Kuwait, beginning the Gulf War.
2003	US-led invasion of Iraq begins.
2008	Burj Khalifa, the tallest building in the world, is built in Dubai.
2011	Arab Spring movements begin.
2015	Jordan passes law to give more power to local authorities

Map of the Region

Economy, Trade, and Resources across the Middle East

Glossary

Bedouin Desert-dwelling nomadic tribes across the Middle East.

brain drain The migration of professionals and skilled workers to foreign countries.

choke point A narrow, dangerous waterway, often used for strategic military purposes.

deficit A net loss of income or other financial means.

expatriate A foreigner who works in another country.

Gross Domestic Product (GDP) The total value of goods and services a country produces.

hajj Islamic holy journey to Mecca; one of the main pillars of Islam.

halal Foods that are permissible for Muslims to eat according to religious law.

hydrocarbon The chemical makeup of oil that allows it to be used for energy.

import-substituting industrialization (ISI) The simultaneous limiting of imports and subsidizing of local businesses to encourage rapid growth in the local economy.

infitah An open-door policy between governments that encourages foreign investment.

inflation The decreasing value of a unit of currency over time.

Islamic Golden Age The period between the eighth and thirteenth centuries when the Islamic world experienced great scientific, economic, and cultural advancements.

Islamist A fundamentalist movement in Islam that is characterized by moral conservatism.

knowledge economy An economy based on informational resources other than natural resources.

Kurds A mainly Islamic group of people living in Kurdistan; people who are ethnically distinct from Arabs.

laissez-faire A social or political attitude that allows things to take their own course, without intervention.

modernization Maintaining a level of education, technology, and infrastructure that allows a nation to participate in a global economy.

nationalism The patriotic loyalty to one nation over another.

Ottoman Empire Turkish Empire founded by Sultan Osman that lasted from roughly 1300 to 1914.

philanthropic Charitable.

power vacuum An opening in a nation or region's political leadership that allows for another nation to take over.

subsidizing Financial assistance, usually by a government, for necessary businesses that may not initially make enough money to operate independently.

Sykes-Picot Agreement The secret agreement between England and France to divide the Middle Eastern territories taken from the Ottoman Empire at the end of World War I.

westernization Emulating Western culture and beliefs.

Further Information

Books

Allan, J.A. *The Middle East Water Question: Hydropolitics and the Global Economy.* London, UK: I.B. Tauris, 2000.

Ansah, Hassan. *Life, Death, and Community in Cairo's City of the Dead.* Bloomington, IN: iUniverse, 2010.

Chaudhry, Kiren Aziz. *Price of Wealth: Economies and Institutions in the Middle East.* Ithaca, NY: Cornell University Press, 1997.

Danahar, Paul. *The New Middle East: The World After the Arab Spring.* London, UK: Bloomsbury Paperbacks, 2013.

Fromkin, David. *A Peace to End All Peace: The Fall of the Ottoman Empire and Creation of the Modern Middle East.* New York: Holt Paperbacks, 2009.

Websites

His Majesty King Abdullah II

http://kingabdullah.jo

His Majesty King Abdullah II of Jordan's website details the king's important initiatives for the burgeoning country. The site also gives information about the king's plans for maintaining peaceful relations with Jordan's neighbors and nations in the West.

Middle East Info

http://www.middle-east-info.org

This website's mission is to "promote democracy, pluralism, and mutual respect in the Middle East" by providing information gathered from Middle Eastern nations.

US-Middle East Partnership Initiative (MEPI)

http://mepi.state.gov

The state department's website outlines how young people can get involved in a cross-cultural exchange program with the Middle East through MEPI programming.

Bibliography

Abderrahim-Ben Salah, Kaouther. "Libya." *African Economic Outlook*, 2015. Accessed May 24, 2016. http://www.africaneconomicoutlook.org/sites/default/files/2016-05/eBook_AEO2016.pdf.

Butterworth, Lisa. "Etsy Around the World: Israel." *The Etsy Blog*. March 10, 2014. https://blog.etsy.com/en/etsy-around-the-world-a-visit-to-israel.

Clinch, Matt, and Hadley Gamble. "Saudi Arabia Unveils 15-year Plan to Transform Its Economy." *CNBC*. April 25, 2016. http://www.cnbc.com/2016/04/25/saudi-arabias-government-officially-unveils-long-term-economic-plan.html.

Cochran, Judith, Mona Nabhani, Rima Bahous, and Rewa Zeinati. "Leadership in the Middle East: The Story of Women in Lebanon." *Middle East Institute*. October 13, 2010. http://www.mei.edu/content/leadership-middle-east-story-women-lebanon.

"The Economic Outlook for the Middle East and North Africa." *The World Bank*. October 5, 2015. http://www.worldbank.org/en/region/mena/brief/economic-outlook-middle-east-and-north-africa-october-2015.

"Economics: It's More Than Oil." *PBS*. Accessed May 10, 2016. http://www.pbslearningmedia.org/resource/arct14.soc.gcmeeco/economics-its-more-than-oil.

Freeman, Colin. "Taking in Syria's Migrants." *The Telegraph.*
September 14, 2015. http://www.telegraph.co.uk/news/
worldnews/middleeast/syria/11864804/Taking-in-Syrias-
migrants-may-be-merciful-but-will-add-to-its-crippling-
brain-drain.html.

Friedman, Matti. "What the Media Gets Wrong about Israel."
The Atlantic. November 30, 2014. http://www.theatlantic.
com/international/archive/2014/11/how-the-media-makes-
the-israel-story/383262.

Goldman, Michal. "Nasser's Republic: The Making of
Modern Egypt." *PBS.* Accessed June 5, 2016. http://
pbsinternational.org/programs/nassers-republic-the-
making-of-modern-egypt.

"HM King Abdullah II Ibn al-Hussein." *The Muslim 500.* 2016.
http://themuslim500.com/profile/king-abdullah-ii-jordan.

"Iran Overview." *The World Bank.* April 1, 2016. http://www.
worldbank.org/en/country/iran/overview.

Keough, Peter. "Works of Three Local Documentarians to
Be Screened at IFFBoston" *Boston Globe.* April 22, 2016.
https://www.bostonglobe.com/arts/movies/2016/04/21/
works-three-local-documentarians-screened-iffboston/
ENsYiMwCdRtOV1oTQX0LpI/story.html.

Kuran, Timur. "Why the Middle East Is Economically
Underdeveloped: Historical Mechanisms of Institutional
Stagnation." *The Journal of Economic Perspectives,* Vol. 18,
No. 3 (Summer, 2004), pp. 71-90. https://econ.duke.

edu/uploads/assets/People/Kuran/Why%20ME%20
underdeveloped.pdf.

Learner, Miri. "Israeli Women Entrepreneurs: An Examination of Factors Affecting Performance." *Journal of Business Venturing*, 124(4):315-339, June 1997. https://www. researchgate.net/publication/223836012_Israeli_Women_ Entrepreneurs_An_Examination_of_Factors_Affecting_ Performance.

"Libya." 2016 Index of Economic Freedom. *The Heritage Foundation*. Accessed June 1, 2016. http://www.heritage. org/index/country/Libya.

McNamara, Alix, and Caroline Howard, eds. "The World's 100 Most Powerful Women." *Forbes*. 2016. http://www.forbes. com/power-women.

"Morocco." 2016 Index of Economic Freedom. *The Heritage Foundation*, 2016. Accessed May 10, 2016. http://www. heritage.org/index/country/morocco.

Osman, Tarek. "Why Border Lines Drawn with a Ruler in WW1 Still Rock the Middle East." *BBC News*. December 14, 2013. http://www.bbc.com/news/world-middle-east-25299553.

Pace, Eric. "Habib Bourguiba, Independence Champion and President of Tunisia, Dies at 96." *New York Times*. April 7, 2000. http://www.nytimes.com/2000/04/07/world/habib-bourguiba-independence-champion-and-president-of-tunisia-dies-at-96.html.

"Redefining Entrepreneurship: Etsy Sellers' Economic Impact." *Etsy.* 2013. http://extfiles.etsy.com/Press/reports/Etsy_RedefiningEntrepreneurshipReport_2013.pdf.

Roubini, Nouriel. "The Middle East Meltdown and Its Global Economic Risk." *The Guardian.* https://www.theguardian.com/business/2015/oct/01/the-middle-east-meltdown-and-its-global-economic-risk.

Scheinmann, Gabriel. "The Map That Ruined the Middle East." *The Tower.* July 2013. http://www.thetower.org/article/the-map-that-ruined-the-middle-east.

Singh, Michael. "The Real Middle East Crisis Is Economic." *New York Times.* August 19, 2014. http://www.nytimes.com/2014/08/20/opinion/the-real-middle-east-crisis-is-economic.html.

Trueman, C.N. "Gamal Abdel Nasser." *History Learning Site.* May 26, 2015. http://www.historylearningsite.co.uk/modern-world-history-1918-to-1980/the-middle-east-1917-to-1973/gamal-abdel-nasser.

"The World Factbook: Bahrain." *Central Intelligence Agency.* July 12, 2016. https://www.cia.gov/library/publications/the-world-factbook/geos/ba.html.

Wright, Robin. "Imagining a Remapped Middle East." *New York Times.* September 28, 2013. http://www.nytimes.com/2013/09/29/opinion/sunday/imagining-a-remapped-middle-east.html.

Index

Page numbers in **boldface** are illustrations. Entries in **boldface** are glossary terms.

Abdullah II (king), 86–88, **87**
Algeria, 14–15, 71–73
Arab Spring protests, 68, 77

Bahrain, 13, 28–29
Bedouin, 45
Bourguiba, Habib Ben Ali, 15, 88–92, **89**
brain drain, 13, 49

choke point, 39, 48

deficit, 50
Dubai, 12, 47–48

Egypt, 14, 53–55
expatriate, 7, 12, 28, 38, 43, 44, 45, 46

Ferdinand, Archduke Franz, 16
figure head, 93

Golden Age of Islam, 16
Gross Domestic Product (GDP), 34, 37, 57
gross national income (GNI), 6
Gulf region, 12, 27, 84
Gulf War, 30–31, 39

hajj, 16, 32
halal, 43–44
handcrafted businesses, 63
Hussein, Saddam, **30**, 31, 36
hydrocarbon, 7, 13, 35, 72, 75

import-substituting industrialization (ISI), 24
infitah, 24
inflation, 37
Iran, 7, 12, 13, 23, 27, 32–35
Iraq, 7, 12, 27, 31, 36–37, 38
Islamic Golden Age, 32, **33**
Islamist, 50
Israel, 14, 25, 60–62, 92, 96
Jordan, 14, 56–57

knowledge economy, 57
Kurds, 36
Kuwait, 38–39

laissez-faire, 60
Lebanon, 57–60
Levant region, the, 14, 53, 86
Libya, 73–75

modernization, 6, 20–21, 32, 39, 42, 80
Morocco, 9, 12, 14, 71, 75–78

Nasser, Gamal Abdel, 18, 74, 83, 92–97, **93**
nationalism, 18, 23, 97
North Africa, 14, 71, 88

Obama, Barack, 11
Oman, 27, 39–41, 46
Ottoman Empire, 15, 16, 23, 32, 54, 56, 57, 78, 86

Palestine, 62–67
Persian Constitutional Revolution, 34
philanthropic commitments, 86
power vacuum, 16

Qaddafi, Colonel Muammar, 74–75, **82**, 83
Qasimi, Sheikh Lubna al-, 84–86, **85**
Qatar, 12, 27, 41–44

Saudi Arabia, 44–45
Six-Day War, 56, 60, 66, 96
subsidizing industries, 24
Sykes-Picot Agreement/map, 10, 17–18
Syria, 67–69

Tunisia, 15, 78–79

United Arab Emirates (UAE), 12, 27, 46–48, 50, 84
US–Middle East Partnership Initiative (MEPI), 22

war economy, 68
water-desalinization, 39, 45
westernization, 20–21, 25
women, in the Middle East, 80–81
World Wars I / II, 15–16, 20, 68

Yemen, 12, 48–51

About the Author

Tatiana Ryckman is a writer, editor, and teacher from Cleveland, Ohio. She received a master's degree in creative writing from Vermont College of Fine Arts and currently resides in Austin, Texas. Her publications include *Oprah Winfrey: Media Mogul and Philanthropist* and *Alexander Hamilton: The First Secretary of the Treasury and an Author of the Federalist Papers*, as well as a collection of short stories called *Twenty-Something*. When she is not writing she enjoys eating tacos, reading, and bicycling with friends.